Hanna-Barbera's
Prime Time Cartoons

Raymond Valinoti, Jr.

BearManor
Media

Orlando, Florida

Published in the USA by
BearManor Media
1317 Edgewater Dr. #110
Orlando, FL 32804
www.BearManorMedia.com

Softcover Edition
ISBN: 978-1-62933-588-9

Printed in the United States of America

Table of Contents

Introduction

On June 20, 1960, Hanna-Barbera's animated television series *The Huckleberry Hound Show* won an Emmy for Outstanding Children's Program. The show had been successfully syndicated on the airwaves since the fall of 1958. Each episode consisted of three cartoons, one starring the titular blue hued, easygoing canine, another starring a sardonic cat named Jinks and his nemeses, two plucky mice called Pixie and Dixie, and the third starring a conniving animal who answered to the name Yogi Bear.

Although *The Huckleberry Hound Show* was officially a children's program, it was popular with adults as well. The characters, expertly voiced by actors Daws Butler and Don Messick, had the same appeal to all ages as did theatrical cartoon characters like Bugs Bunny and Mr. Magoo. Huckleberry Hound and his fellow toons were as endearing and as funny as live action performers like Jack Benny and Red Skelton. The situations the cartoon characters got into were often amusing and even when the material wasn't up to par, viewers remained entertained, because of the stars' strong personalities.

The Huckleberry Hound Show was especially popular in bars. It became a ritual for patrons all over the United States to stop chatting the moment the program appeared on the screen. Patrons of one bar in Seattle, Washington couldn't ignore a sign posted on Thursday evenings between 6 and 6:30 PM: "No loud tinkling of glasses. No unnecessary conversation. No disturbing elements. No drinks served. BECAUSE WE'RE WATCHING HUCKLEBERRY HOUND."

The Huckleberry Hound Show was the first full-length television cartoon program produced by William Hanna and Joe Barbera. (The producers had previously worked on *Ruff and Reddy*, animated segments of a live-action children's TV program.) In 1959, they devised another ostensible children's program that was even more sophisticated, *The Quick Draw McGraw Show*. Like the previous show, each episode consisted of three cartoons with different characters. Unlike *Huckleberry Hound*'s segments, which consisted of a random variety of comical situations, *Quick Draw McGraw*'s segments lampooned popular live-action TV genres. Quick Draw McGraw, a brave but lunkheaded horse sheriff, skewered Westerns. Snooper and Blabber, a cat and mouse sleuthing team, burlesqued detective shows. And Auggie Doggie, a puppy, and his father Doggy Daddy spoofed sitcom families. (As with live action sitcoms like *My Three Sons*, the mother was absent.)

The Quick Draw McGraw Show entertained viewers ranging from toddlers to senior citizens. The show seemed even more popular with adults than with children; according to a National Enterprise Association column, viewers were "reported to be 60 per cent adult." The critics also loved the program, particularly appreciating the satire. One reviewer, Bob Blackburn, opined, "[The program] encourages the kids to develop a good sound derision for all the junk they see on TV."

But although Hanna-Barbera spoofed TV conventions, the studio harbored no visions of revolutionizing the medium. What mattered to the studio was creating profitable shows that everyone could enjoy. And Hanna-Barbera's distributor, Screen Gems, the television branch of the venerable theatrical studio Columbia Pictures, was delighted with the results. Why shouldn't Hanna-Barbera develop a new program for primetime, one specifically marketed for both children *and* adults? The head of Screen Gems's sales department, John Mitchell, suggested this to Bill Hanna and Joe Barbera. Bill and Joe immediately agreed and set to work on their first primetime series.

The results of Hanna-Barbera's labors, *The Flintstones*, premiered on ABC on September 30, 1960. It was by no means the first animated primetime TV series but it had an intriguing concept - a prehistoric couple and their neighbors engaged in sitcomish shenanigans tailored to their antediluvian setting. One specific live action sitcom served as a blueprint for *The Flintstones*'s format - *The Honeymooners* starring Jackie Gleason as blustery bus driver Ralph Kramden. Bill Hanna later told author Ted Sennett: "I used to watch *The Honeymooners* and laugh until tears would run down my cheeks." He and Joe Barbera were determined to provoke the same reaction to *The Flintstones* from viewers.

Despite initial pans from the critics, Bill and Joe succeeded. *The Flintstones* was incredibly successful, lasting for six seasons. Even the press eventually warmed up to the show. Inevitably, the production people at ABC demanded that Hanna-Barbera produce more animated primetime product. In the fall of 1961, *Top Cat*, about a scheming alley cat who tries to outwit a human cop, premiered. Bill and Joe used another live-action sitcom as a template for the new show, *The Phil Silvers Show*. Then in the fall of 1962, Hanna-Barbera came out with *The Jetsons*, about a family living in an imaginary future civilization. Two years later, *Jonny Quest* hit ABC's airwaves. Unlike the other cartoon shows, this one was a serious adventure program. Hanna-Barbera seemed prolific in the primetime field.

But none of the shows in the wake of *The Flintstones* lasted beyond a single season. Eventually, Hanna-Barbera abandoned the evening market to focus on Saturday morning kidvid. Bill and Joe attempted to return to primetime in the fall of 1968 with *The New Adventures of Huckleberry Finn* on NBC. A purported sequel to Mark Twain's classic book, it was another serious adventure that combined animation with live-action. But this show also bit the dust after one season.

Why did Bill and Joe ultimately flounder in primetime programming? There is no easy answer. This book will explain how each of the cited shows evolved, will examine how Hanna-Barbera's PR department promoted them and analyze the public and critical feedback at the time they originally ran. Each show will be given critical appraisal, determining how they hold up half a century later.

The Flintstones

Broadcast Station: ABC. Telecast: September 30, 1960-September 2, 1966. Studio: Hanna-Barbera/Screen Gems. Produced, directed and written by William Hanna and Joseph Barbera. Episodes directed by Alex Lovy and Charles A. Nichols, among others. Written by Michael Maltese, Ralph Goodman, Warren Foster, R. Allen Safian, Barry Blitzer, Tony Benedict, Herb Finn, Jack Raymond, Sid Zelinka, Arthur Phillips, Joanna Lee, Bill Idelson, Rance Howard, Phil Hahn, Jack Hanrahan, R.S. Allen, and Harvey Bullock, among others. Music by Hoyt Curtin. Voices: Alan Reed (Fred Flintstone); Mel Blanc, Daws Butler (Barney Rubble); Jean Vander Pyl (Wilma Flintsone/Pebbles Flintstone); Bea Benaderet, Gerry Johnson (Betty Rubble); John Stephenson (Mr. Slate/others); Don Messick (Bamm Bamm/Arnold the Newsboy/others); Verna Felton, Janet Waldo (Wilma's Mother); Harvey Korman (The Great Gazoo); and Hal Smith, Jerry Mann, Walker Edmiston, Herb Vigran, Herschel Bernardi, Howard McNear, Frank Nelson, June Foray, Howard Morris, Naomi Lewis, Paula Winslowe, Jerry Hausner, Leo DeLyon, Paul Frees, and Sam Edwards, among others.

In later years, Joe Barbera would claim that it took eight frustrating weeks for Hanna-Barbera to find a sponsor for *The Flintstones*. The struggle took place in New York City, where most of the television and agency people would meet to negotiate in the late 1950s and early 1960s. In a 1997 interview, he went into elaborate detail about promoting the show to potential advertisers in his hotel room with storyboards for two proposed episodes: "From the window, I could see Central Park...and when I started with this pitch, it was covered with snow. Gradually, over eight weeks, I saw the snow disappear. I saw the swans come back. I saw the trees begin to bud. Eight weeks there..." Finally on the last day of the eighth week, before Joe was scheduled to fly back to California, executives at ABC accepted his proposal and bought the show. In the same 1997 interview, Barbera dramatically stated: "Thank goodness because if it wasn't for them [the ABC executives], this was the last day, and I was slated to get on the plane at noon, and if they hadn't bought it, I would have taken everything back, put it in storage. And you never come back next year with it. You never try to repeat a show and sell it because it doesn't work; they say, 'We saw that.' "

One would like to believe this account is true. What a compelling tale-Joe Barbera struggled to make the concept of *The Flintstones*, which would become one of the most beloved television shows of all time, turn into a reality- and he nearly failed. But we know from contemporary press items that it was relatively easy for Hanna-Barbera to get *The Flintstones* off the ground. The first published announcement that the cartoon would soon hit the airwaves was ten days after the first official day of winter in 1959, so Joe Barbera and company didn't have to wait for the snow to disappear.

Casting for the voices of the principal characters on *The Flintstones* was more difficult. Daws Butler, already voicing such popular Hanna-Barbera characters like Huckleberry Hound and Quick Draw McGraw, was the first choice to provide dialogue for Fred Flintstone. But Bill and Joe worried about overusing him so they searched the talent pool for experienced radio and cartoon voice actors. Bill Thompson, the voice of Mr. Wallace Whipple on the radio hit *Fibber McGee and Molly* and of the dog Droopy in Tex Avery-directed

MGM cartoons, auditioned for the role but he had trouble utilizing the low end of his voice for Fred Flintstone. Hanna and Barbera felt Thompson could not adequately convey the character's lovable gruffness- the same quality in Jackie Gleason's Ralph Kramden. (Thompson would later voice a children's cartoon character for Hanna-Barbera, Touche' Turtle.)

Alan Reed succeeded where Thompson failed. For years on both radio and in live-action films, the veteran actor had excelled at articulating rough hewn characters such as Finnegan and Clancy the Cop, both on the popular radio sitcom *Duffy's Tavern*. The character of Fred Flintstone would be Reed's most famous role. The actor not only voiced him throughout *The Flintstones's* considerable run, but in revivals and commercials until his death in 1977. It was Reed who devised Fred's catchphrase "Yabba Dabba Doo!"

Daws Butler was also the first choice for Fred Flintstone's bosom buddy Barney Rubble but was dropped for the same reason he was dropped for the part of Fred. Hal Smith, who was prolific in cartoons and live action television and films, tried out for the role of Barney. But Bill and Joe decided that Smith wasn't right for the role. Mel Blanc, the legendary Man of a Thousand Voices, who had already done a variety of radio and theatrical cartoon work from the Maxwell, Jack Benny's broken down automobile, to Bugs Bunny, won the part of Barney. (Being the multi-faceted actor that he was, Blanc also did other voices on *The Flintstones*, including Fred's pet dinosaur Dino and would do countless voices on other Hanna-Barbera cartoons until he passed away in 1989.)

Much of the humor in *The Honeymooners* was derived from marital situations, particularly arguments. Since *The Flintstones's* format was derived from Jackie Gleason's earlier show, wives would be major characters. Jean Vander Pyl, already doing voices for Hanna-Barbera cartoons, was hired to play Fred's wife Wilma while Bea Benaderet got the job as Barney's wife Betty. Both Vander Pyl and Benaderet were versatile actresses and would provide other voices on *The Flintstones*. Vander Pyl would provide babbling and other baby sounds for the Flintstones' little daughter Pebbles in later episodes.

3

When Bill and Joe first conceived their primetime series, *The Flintstones* was not the original title. Hanna and Barbera considered *The Flagstones* but then realized that surname was too similar to Flagston, the surname of Mort Walker's popular comic strip couple *Hi and Lois*. *The Gladstones* was proposed but that name sounded too much like Gladstone Gander, a major character in Donald Duck comic books. In retrospect, it's hard to comprehend why Bill and Joe didn't decide on the name Flintstone in the first place; the combination of the words *flint* and *stone* perfectly evoke the show's Stone Age setting.

With the name and cast set in stone (pardon the pun), Bill and Joe launched a blitzkrieg of PR declaring the coming of a sophisticated animated series especially for adults. They announced that *The Flintstones* would be more than just a comedy; it would be, they claimed, "a satire on modern suburban life." The brass at ABC eagerly supported the hype. ABC's President Oliver Treyz even told the press that *The Flintstones* was "A sensational development...it'll start a landslide...the biggest thing in TV programming that the free world has ever seen..." Treyz even professed concern that the show's humor would be *too* sophisticated for the average viewer: "...the only thing we've got to worry about is whether we get too egg-head. Some of those jokes get a bit, ah, esoteric..."

Hanna and Barbera were determined to market *The Flintstones* for adults. One of the sponsors happened to be Winston Cigarettes. Animated commercials were devised showing the Flintstones and the Rubbles plugging these tobacco products. (The other sponsor was One-a-Day Vitamins manufactured by Miles Laboratories. Miles would later devise chewable Flintstones Vitamins for children.)

The suits at ABC decided that since *The Flintstones* was a primetime sitcom, it should have a laugh track like other primetime sitcoms. Bill and Joe had reservations about using canned laughter. Hanna told reporter Hal Humphrey, "It simply never occurred to us that laughs were something which had to be added." None of Bill and Joe's previous made-for-TV cartoon product had laugh tracks. (They weren't marketed as primetime sitcoms so laugh tracks weren't requested.) But Bill and Joe, eager to get *The Flintstones* on the air, agreed to use them. They were determined, however, not to let the canned laughter get in the way of the cartoons' actual humor. They tested and rejected two proposed laugh tracks. Joe Barbera told Humphrey, "They were too heavy and just didn't work. Now we have a much lighter track, which we hope the audience will be aware of only subconsciously."

Up until the premiere of *The Flintstones*, Hanna-Barbera's television cartoons were critics' darlings. But reviewers were underwhelmed by the first episode, "The Flintstone Flyer." They looked forward to a hilarious lampoon of human mores but discovered the episode was a conventional comedy set up- Fred and Barney try to escape going to the opera with their wives so they can go bowling. A typical pan came from Jack Gould in the New York *Times*: "Where it was presumed a Stone Age perspective would be applied to civilization's contemporary foibles, the thirty-minute cartoon turned out to be an extremely heavy-handed and labored effort. The humor was of the boff-and-sock genre, nothing light or subtle."

But unimpressed critics could not discourage the public from watching *The Flintstones*. They marveled at the cartoon's clever gags utilizing prehistoric creatures as mechanical devices. For example, a mammoth's trunk functioned as a vacuum cleaner and a gluttonous pig served as a garbage disposal. Bill Hanna in his autobiography noted that the humor of these devices were derived from the nonchalant way the humans utilized critters as utensils and machines. He pointed out, "Fred, Wilma, Barney, and Betty all played the Stone Age gimmicks for laughs, but they generally did it with straight faces that were often so dead pan that they would have made Buster Keaton proud."

Enhancing the laughs were the animals' reactions to their dilemmas. They weren't exactly overjoyed to be used by humans as tools. In one episode, Fred and Barney decide to make a record for Wilma and Betty but in the recording booth, they're suddenly tongue-tied. A bird, functioning as a phonograph needle (this show was aired long before digital recording came into existence), gripes, "Oh brother, every customer, the same thing. They want to make a record but they don't know what to say." After making a few suggestions to

5

Fred and Barney, the bird bemoans, "Come on, fellows. I was taking a bath when you came in."

But if all *The Flintstones* had to offer were jokes about animals, it wouldn't have succeeded. What kept viewers tuning into to the show was its thoroughly likable characters. Fred and Wilma Flintstone and Barney and Betty Rubble may have been pen and ink drawings but thanks to the adroit scripting and the actors' impressive voiceover work, they were as credible and identifiable as actual human beings. Conceptually, Fred Flintstone may have been a knockoff of Jackie Gleason's Ralph Kramden, but Alan Reed avoided a blatant Gleason impersonation, drawing on his own previous voice work. He not only made Fred Flintstone a distinctive character in his own right, but also gave him depth- an outward bluster that hid an inner vulnerability.

When voicing Barney Rubble, Mel Blanc did not ape Art Carney, who had played Kramden's sidekick Ed Norton. In the first few episodes, he provided the character with a fairly high-pitched nasal honk. Experimenting with the voice, Blanc eventually altered it to a lower-pitched, smooth tone. His Barney Rubble was a perfect counterpart to Alan Reed's Fred- an easygoing if slightly fuzzy-headed fellow taking everything in stride. Just as Reed's trademark sound of delight was "Yabba Dabba Doo," Blanc's was a giggle: "Eee hee hee hee hee hee."

Jean Vander Pyl's Wilma Flintstone was the ideal mate for Fred despite their quarrels. Like Audrey Meadows as Ralph's wife Alice on *The Honeymooners*, Wilma tried to bring her husband to his senses if he was in a dither or lost in a pipe dream, as she alternated between sarcasm and tenderness. Because of Vander Pyl's heartfelt acting, viewers genuinely believed that she loved Fred despite his faults. Bea Benaderet actually made her Betty Rubble more distinctive than her inspiration, Ed Norton's nondescript wife Trixie. She gave her animated character an appealing squeak that conveyed both wifely devotion and an acute perception of what made her husband tick. Benaderet even gave her laugh a chirpy titter.

Another asset for *The Flintstones* was Hoyt Curtin's peppy musical score. Curtin had been composing for Hanna-Barbera's television cartoons ever since they began production in 1957. A zealous fan of big band music, he infused the program's *Flintstones* score with a jazzy sound. This upbeat approach suited Bill and Joe just fine. Curtin later recalled Hanna and Barbera's musical concepts: "Their idea was to write a piece of music that's happy. These cartoons are not World War Three. They are happy, and if you write a piece of music that's happy, it's pretty much got to go with it. 'Happy' to me is jazz."

Curtin's musical arrangements not only enlivened the program's but enhanced its humor. He created comedic sounds in the instruments, particularly in the contrabassoon, the tuba, and the percussion. Curtin even devised a musical horselaugh, consisting of an eight-note, descending figure for clarinets and tubas. This horselaugh was such a potent aural punctuation to gags that a laughtrack wasn't necessary.

Curtin also composed the music for the program's memorable theme song "Meet the Flintstones." (Bill worked on the lyrics.) For the first two seasons, *The Flintstones* had a different theme song, "Rise and Shine." The familiar "Meet the Flintstones" originated as background music, composed in a Dixieland style. In the second season, Curtin reminisced, the music was altered "to a more 'caveman' sound. I had all the timpanists in town. It was like Swiss bell ringers, you play this note and you play that." In the third season, lyrics were added to the song with the same "caveman" sound. Curtin hired a jazz band and some singers to record the new version.

But let us go back to the first season. By the time it ended, *The Flintstones's* Nielsen ratings were quite high, ranking at 18 among all programs. According to Thomas J. Fleming in a *Saturday Evening Post* article on the show, teenagers in particular enjoyed watching it. The show was also garnering some prestige, winning a Golden Globe for outstanding achievement in international televison cartoons and receiving an Emmy nomination. The publication *TV-Radio Mirror* voted *The Flintstones* the most original series. And the National Cartoonists Society honored Bill and Joe with a Silver Plaque as the best animators of 1960. Not surprisingly, the show was renewed for another season. Bill and Joe must have felt vindicated after enduring tepid reviews.

But just after the voiceover sessions were wrapped up for the first season, disaster struck. On January 24, 1961, the voice of Barney Rubble, Mel Blanc, was driving his sports car on Sunset Boulevard to work on a television commercial. Suddenly, another car, operated by a Menlo College student, smashed head-on into Blanc's car. The collision nearly killed Blanc. The Man of a Thousand Voices suffered multiple fractures and head injuries, rendering him comatose.

Miraculously, Blanc soon regained consciousness and began to recover. But the healing process was slow and agonizing. He was unable to work on voiceover sessions for five episodes in the second season. Daws Butler subbed for Blanc at these sessions, coming off like a low-key Ed Norton. (He avoided sounding *exactly* like Carney's Ed Norton to prevent any lawsuit.) When Blanc was released from the hospital, he resumed voicework for Barney Rubble. Still struggling to recover, Mel was bedridden and bandaged from chest to foot. Instead of going to the recording studio, the recording studio went to him. Sound equipment was set up in Blanc's home so he could record his lines. Blanc later recalled in his autobiography:

> The first time we taped the show at my home, it was quite a chaotic scene. Tangles of wires were scattered all over the floor, and chairs and microphones were arranged around my hospital bed. A speaker had been mounted on the wall so that [my son] Noel and producer Joe Barbera could communicate to the actors from the makeshift control room....
>
> "Hope you're comfortable, Mel." Barbera's voice came cracking over the speaker, "We're in for a long evening." He wasn't kidding. Every couple of hours Joe would ask if I was too tired to carry on, but I insisted on completing the show.

Blanc continued these arduous sessions for months. Despite the difficulties, Mel found them a welcome respite from the boredom of lying in bed all day. The sessions also boosted his morale, speeding his recovery.

Eventually, Blanc regained his mobility and he could go to the recording studio again.

As Blanc recuperated, *The Flintstones* continued to do well in the ratings. The show was renewed for a third season and then a fourth. It seemed that it would run forever. Critics also warmed up to the show. Brooks Atkinson in the New York *Times*, the same publication where Jack Gould panned the show's first episode, wrote a laudatory column on October 4, 1963: "No actor could duplicate the exuberant frenzy of Fred Flintstone, the Stone Age extrovert whose combination of bullheadedness and blundering... is the weekly topic of a remarkably fresh cartoon...Thanks to the raciness of the cartoon medium, [Fred Flintstone and Barney Rubble] are worth a hundred of the standard [live-action] comedies, and they make [live-action] actors look inept and anxious."

At the time Atkinson wrote this, *The Flintstones*'s format had undergone a significant change. For the show's first two seasons, the show focused on adult-oriented themes, particularly Fred and Barney's attempts to sneak away from their wives so they could have their own fun. Neither the Flintstones nor the Rubbles had any children. (When *The Flintstones* was first conceived, the staff considered giving Fred and Wilma a son called Fred, Jr. but they decided that, like the Kramdens, the Flintstones would be childless.) But at the end of a third season episode, "The Surprise," aired on January 25, 1963, Wilma told Fred she was expecting a baby. It was the first time an animated character announced her pregnancy on television. The following three episodes comically dealt with Fred's efforts to prepare for his upcoming fatherhood. Then on the February 22nd episode "Dress Rehearsal," Wilma gave birth to a girl named Pebbles.

Hanna-Barbera's decision to make Fred and Wilma parents was not entirely artistic. At the time of Pebbles' "birth," a company called Ideal Toys was manufacturing dolls of *The Flintstones* characters. The addition of a baby to the show meant the production of a new doll. The baby's gender was female because Ideal Toys believed that girl dolls would sell more than boy dolls. Pebbles' arrival gave Fred Flintstone a good reason to stay home rather than go out on the town. Hanna-Barbera provided new scenarios dealing with Fred and Wilma's efforts to raise the baby, with the help of Barney and Betty. Thus *The Flintstones* became more family friendly. This was especially evident with the show's new sponsors: Winston Cigarettes cut ties with the program the same year of Pebbles' debut, to be replaced by Welch's Grape Juice and Skippy Peanut Butter.

The show's scenarists successfully devised funny episodes dealing with Fred's fatherhood in the third and fourth seasons. One particularly riotous episode, "Reel Trouble," focused on Fred's passion for making and showing home movies of Pebbles doing every trivial thing, to the annoyance of the viewers. Before long, Barney and Betty became parents, adopting a baby boy called Bamm Bamm. Bamm Bamm was a one-joke character (the little tyke was amazingly strong) but he didn't hurt the show.

But at the end of the 1963-64 season, Bea Benaderet was unceremoniously dropped as the voice of Betty Rubble. At this time, she was a regular on the live-action TV show *Petticoat Junction* and a *Variety* column reported she couldn't fully commit to *The Flintstones*. But Jean Vander Pyl told TV historian Stu Shostak that Benaderet's replacement Gerry Johnson was Joe Barbera's girlfriend. Nobody at Hanna-Barbera told Bea she was replaced; she only learned this when Jean phoned her to inquire about her absence from the voiceover sessions.

Gerry Johnson was a weak replacement for Bea Benaderet. Although she somewhat sounded like her predecessor, she lacked Bea's innate warmth and sharpness. In other words, Gerry Johnson's Betty Rubble was a pale imitation. But even if Benaderet had stayed on, the show's fifth season would still have had problems. For the first time, ratings were down. The live-action sitcom *The Munsters* debuted on CBS that season in *The Flintstones*'s time slot and it was drawing viewers away. (Ironically one of the season's episodes, "The Gruesomes," spotlighted a family of friendly monsters- just like CBS's *Munsters*.)

The Munsters may have seemed fresh to the public since popular creatures like the Frankenstein Monster and Dracula were never used in a sitcom before.

10

Or maybe people felt *The Flintstones* was beginning to get stale. Whatever the reason for the cartoon's declining ratings, ABC responded in December 1964 by giving *The Flintstones* a new time slot. This maneuver worked: *The Flintstones's* ratings not only recovered, but the show was renewed for another season. (Another Hanna-Barbera primetime cartoon, *Jonny Quest*, replaced the show in the time slot opposite *The Munsters*. This show was not renewed. There will be more about *Jonny Quest* in a subsequent chapter.)

By the end of the 1964-65 season, *The Flintstones'* s storylines were focusing less on everyday happenings and more on fantasy events. In one episode, the Flintstones and the Rubbles even traveled to the future in a time machine. The program was still entertaining but the scenarists started to run out of ideas centering on predicaments viewers could identify with, such as Fred trying to get a raise or going on a diet. Of course, these dilemmas took place in an imagined prehistoric setting but people could still empathize with the characters' frustrations. By getting involved more in completely unreal adventures, the Flintstones and the Rubbles were becoming less relatable.

In the 1965-66 season, *The Flintstones* plunged further into the fantastic with the creation of a new character the Great Gazoo. He was a tiny alien from the future assigned by his planet to examine the behavior of prehistoric Earthlings. Fred and Barney were the only adult Earthlings who could see and hear Gazoo. The alien was condescending, addressing them as "Dum Dums." Gazoo used his extraterrestrial powers to fulfill Fred and Barney's wishes but the results went awry and Gazoo would promptly undo these wishes. Gazoo intended for the results to go awry to convince Fred and Barney to be satisfied with their lot. Voiced by Harvey Korman, the Great Gazoo was amusingly smug. But it was disconcerting to see likable protagonists like Fred and Barney reduced to being stooges for a supercilious alien. The show's ratings began to suffer again. At the end of the 1965-66 season, ABC pulled the plug on *The Flintstones*.

Like other long-running network shows, *The Flintstones* was rerun in local syndication. Not only were the reruns popular but they were even more profitable for Hanna-Barbera than the initial network airings. As of this moment, the episodes are still run on television and are available for purchase and rental on home video and for streaming. And after more than half a century, the episodes still hold up well. Fred Flintstone and Barney Rubble in particular remain funny and appealing because they still resonate with today's viewers. As Yowp pointed out in a 2010 blog entry "The Flintstones' 50th Birthday": "They behave in a way we all recognise. Who doesn't know at least a toned-down version of a loud guy who thinks he has all the answers but, at the same time, has a softer side he doesn't like showing? Or a friend who's happy-go-lucky, if not a little goofy?" As long as such people exist, audiences will always enjoy *The Flintstones*.

The ABC network brass knew at the end of the 1960-61 season that people enjoyed *The Flintstones*. If an animated primetime series could be successful, they thought, there was no reason why another animated primetime series couldn't be devised. The executives were so eager for Hanna-Barbera to create another show that Joe Barbera persuaded them to produce it on the basis of a single drawing of a cat. This cat would be the titular star of *Top Cat*. Like *The Flintstones*, *Top Cat* would be derived from a live-action sitcom. In this case, the sitcom was *The Phil Silvers Show*.

Episode Guide for *The Flintstones*

Season 1 (1960–61)

1 "The Flintstone Flyer" Airdate: September 30, 1960

One evening, Fred pretends to be sick so he and Barney can go bowling instead of taking their wives to the opera. The men use Barney's homemade prehistoric helicopter to quickly travel to the bowling alley and then back home before the wives. But Wilma and Betty eventually get wise to Fred and Barney's scheme.

2 "Hot Lips Hannigan" Airdate: October 7, 1960

Fred thinks he can use magic to temporarily get rid of Wilma and Betty. With the wives gone (so he thinks), Fred takes Barney to a nightclub to enjoy trumpeter Hot Lips Hannigan, who happens to be an old friend. The wives show up incognito so they can teach their husbands not to misbehave.

3 "The Swimming Pool" Airdate: October 14, 1960

The construction of a joint swimming pool in the Flintstones' and Rubbles' backyards results in feuding between Fred and Barney. The husbands patch up their differences at Fred's birthday party but while celebrating, Fred inadvertently gets into trouble with the law.

4 "No Help Wanted" Airdate: October 21, 1960

Feeling guilty for unintentionally causing Barney to lose his job, Fred gets a business friend to get Barney hired somewhere else. His new job turns to be a furniture repossessor and his first assignment is to repossess Fred's television. Barney considers it his duty to take away the TV set but Fred doesn't take it well.

Note: Dino makes his debut in this episode.

5 "The Split Personality" Airdate: October 28, 1960

When Fred is struck on the head with a bottle of car polish, he
undergoes a personality change and becomes a cultured gentleman
named "Frederick." At first Wilma is delighted by her husband's
transformation but after a while, she decides she prefers the old rough
mannered Fred.

6 "The Monster from the Tar Pits" Airdate: November 4, 1960

When a Hollyrock film company films its new production *The Monster
from the Tar Pits* in Bedrock, Fred gets a job as a stand-in for star Gary
Granite. This assignment causes him to have delusions of stardom.

7 "The Babysitters" Airdate: November 11, 1960

Even though it means missing a wrestling match, Fred and Barney
reluctantly babysit Wilma's nephew, Egbert. The men watch the match
on television but they experience a blackout in the area. The men
take Egbert to their friend Joe Rockhead's house to see the rest of the
televised bout.

8 "At the Races" Airdate: November 18, 1960

Anxious to raise money so he can open a pool hall, Fred wagers his paycheck
on a slim prospect at the dinosaur racetrack. Fred fibs to Wilma that
a robber beat him up and ran off with the money. His gamble pays off,
but his lie gets him into trouble.

Note: Betty is absent from this episode.

9 "The Engagement Ring" Airdate: November 25, 1960

Wanting to surprise Betty with a belated engagement ring, Barney gives it to Fred to hide. But Wilma finds the gift and is convinced Fred got it for her. He wants to buy a second ring so Wilma won't be disappointed. Lacking the funds, Fred persuades Barney to endure several rounds with a champion boxer to win a $500 prize.

10 "Hollyrock, Here I Come" Airdate: December 2, 1960

Wilma and Betty win a television contest and are awarded with an all-expenses -paid trip to Hollyrock. While on vacation, Wilma wins a part in a television program. Missing their wives, Fred and Barney travel to Hollyrock to see them. Fred winds up getting a part in the same television program and he becomes a prima donna.

11 "The Golf Champion" Airdate: December 9, 1960

Fred wins a trophy in the Loyal Order of Dinosaurs golf tournament. But the club's president Barney won't give him the trophy until he pays his dues. This results in a feud between the husbands and Fred insists Barney return all the items he has borrowed.

12 "The Sweepstakes Ticket" Airdate: December 16, 1960

Fred and Barney buy a sweepstakes ticket and Barney conceals it in the lining of an old coat. When Betty gives the coat away to a passing tramp, Barney and Fred desperately try to retrieve it.

13 "The Drive-In" Airdate: December 23, 1960

Frustrated with their jobs, Fred and Barney buy a drive-in behind Wilma and Betty's backs. Two lovely girls work for them as carhops and when they call Fred and Barney at home, the wives get suspicious.

14 "The Prowler" Airdate: December 30, 1960

In order to protect herself from a prowler at large in Bedrock, Wilma and

Betty take judo lessons. Fred contends that the women would never have the guts to confront a prowler. Determined to validate his claim, he disguises himself one night as a burglar to frighten them. But on that same night, the real prowler appears.

15 "The Girls' Night Out" Airdate: January 6, 1961

Wilma and Betty are complaining that their husbands never take them out, so Fred and Barney treat them to an evening at the amusement park. There, Fred cuts a tune at the recording booth but he loses the record. A group of teenagers find it and give to a DJ. The song not only becomes a hit but Fred becomes a rock star with a new name, "Hi-Fye." "Hi-Fye" tours throughout the town but Wilma and Betty can't stand being constantly on the road. The wives spread a rumor that persuades his fans to reject him.

16 "Arthur Quarry's Dance Class" Airdate: January 13, 1961

Having been invited to a charity ball, Fred and Barney fear they don't have enough class to make a good impression there. In order to redeem themselves as well as spare their wives any embarrassment, the husbands secretly take up dancing lessons at Arthur Quarry's. But the wives suspect them of fooling around with other women.

17 "The Big Bank Robbery" Airdate: January 20, 1961

Fred finds a bag with a lot of money but it turns out the money is stolen. At Wilma and Betty's insistence, he and Barney return the money to the bank but the husbands wind up being accused of the robbery.

18 "The Snorkasaurus Hunter" Airdate: January 27, 1961

The Flintstones and the Rubbles go on vacation in the mountains. There Fred hunts for snorkasauruses and finds one. He winds up adopting him as a pet named Dino.

Note: This episode explains how the Flintstones got Dino. But the dinosaur had appeared as their pet in two earlier episodes, "No Help Wanted" and "Arthur Quarry's Dance Class." Jerry Mann does the voice of an articulate Dino. In subsequent episodes, Dino would be voiced by Mel Blanc and would simply yelp and bark like a dog.

19 "The Hot Piano" Airdate: February 3, 1961

Fred buys a Stoneway piano for Wilma as a present for their 10th wedding anniversary. To his shock, he learns the piano has been stolen.

20 "The Hypnotist" Airdate: February 10, 1961

Fred tries hypnotism and succeeds in making Barney think he's a puppy. But Fred has trouble getting his friend back to normal.

21 "Love Letters on the Rocks" Airdate: February 17, 1961

Fred finds a love poem written for Wilma. Forgetting that he wrote the poem a long time ago when he was courting Wilma, he thinks another man is trying to steal his wife. He hires a detective, Perry Gunnite (a parody of the fictional TV detective Peter Gunn) to expose the culprit. Things get even more awry when Gunnite mistakenly identifies Barney as the home-wrecker.

22 "The Tycoon" Airdate: February 24, 1961

Tired of being insulated in his office, businessman J.L. Gotrocks leaves his job to enjoy the simple pleasures of life. His employees aren't happy about this. When they see Fred and note he looks exactly like their missing boss, they persuade him to take Gotrocks's job. Fred quickly becomes stressed from the monotony of the routine. In the meantime, Gotrocks tries to have fun like ordinary people, but he runs into Wilma, Barney, and Betty, who think he's Fred. Eventually, the two look-a-likes return to their normal situations.

23"The Astra' Nuts" Airdate: March 3, 1961

Fred and Barney plan to undergo an examination for insurance, but they unwittingly enlist in a three-year stint in the Army. As if this predicament isn't outrageous enough, the men get roped into the first lunar-landing mission.

24"The Long, Long Weekend" Airdate: March 10, 1961

A planned vacation in a seaside hotel turns out to be an ordeal when the Flintstones and Rubbles have to work there to fill in for the recently departed staff. To make things more stressful, they're expected to entertain a huge convention.

25"In the Dough" Airdate: March 17, 1961

Wilma and Betty submit their recipe of an "Upside-Down Flint/Rubble Bubble Cake" to a cooking contest and wind up as finalists. But they come down with the measles and are unable to attend the event. Fred and Barney try to win the contest for them by masquerading in drag as their wives.

26"The Good Scout" Airdate: March 24, 1961

Fred is put in charge of a Boy Scout troop and learns the hard way the challenges and perils of this task. An overnight flood strands him and his troop on a tree limb over a waterfall.

27"Rooms for Rent" Airdate: March 31, 1961

Wilma and Betty try to make extra money renting rooms to music students. But the students don't have money. Instead, they teach the wives how to make music and dance for an upcoming talent show.

28"Fred Flintstone: Before and After" Airdate: April 7, 1961

Fred gets a job on a television commercial. Unfortunately for him, he's depicted on the air as the before example of a before-and-after weight loss ad. He receives an offer of a thousand dollars if he can lose 25 pounds in a month. Fred joins an overeaters' support group called "Food Anonymous" to help him slim down and win the money.

Season 2 (1961-62)

29"The Hit Song Writers" Airdate: September 15, 1961

Fred and Barney try to write a song with the help of a shady character, but it turns out to be a rip-off of Hoagy Carmichael's "Stardust." Carmichael, however, discovers a poem of Barney and sets it to music. He treats the Flintstones and the Rubbles to a special dinner where he performs the new song.

Note: Special guest-star Hoagy Carmichael voices his animated likeness and composes the song "Yabba-Dabba-Dabba-Dabba-Doo" for this episode. Daws Butler fills in for an ailing Mel Blanc as the voice of Barney Rubble.

30"Droop-Along Flintstone" Airdate: September 22, 1961

The husbands and the wives look after Cousin Tumbleweed's ranch in the west. Fred and Barney accidentally wander on the movie set of a Western and think the filmed situation is real.

Note: Daws Butler does the voice of Barney.

31"The Missing Bus" Airdate: September 29, 1961

Unhappy with his job at the gravel pits, Fred quits and is hired driving a school bus. But he quickly discovers driving children to and from the school is no breeze.

32"Alvin Brickrock Presents" Airdate: October 6, 1961

Fred is so fascinated by Arnold the paper boy's detective magazine that it goes to his head; he suspects his new neighbor has murdered his wife.

Note: The episode's title is a play on the TV suspense show *Alfred Hitchcock Presents*.

33"Fred Flintstone Woos Again" Airdate: October 13, 1961

When Fred and Wilma go on a second honeymoon, they discover the judge who had married them didn't have a license. This problem could be immediately resolved with another wedding ceremony, but Wilma, recently feeling neglected by Fred, insists he go through the ritual of courting her.

Note: Daws Butler does the voice for Barney.

34"The Rock Quarry Story" Airdate: October 20, 1961

The Hollyrock star Rock Quarry wants to escape from the glamour of fame, so he goes to Bedrock incognito. He fools Fred and Barney, but not Wilma and Betty.

Note: Daws Butler does the voice for Barney.

35"The Soft Touchables" Airdate: October 27, 1961

Aspiring detectives Fred and Barney want to solve crimes but they get into hot water with crooks *and* the law.

Note: The title is a play on the TV crime series *The Untouchables*.

36"Flintstone of Prinstone" Airdate: November 3, 1961

Desiring a raise at work, Fred starts attending Prinstone University's night accounting classes but he somehow becomes quarterback for the school's football team.

37 "The Little White Lie" Airdate: November 10, 1961

Fred wins in a poker game but he doesn't want Wilma to know about his gambling. When she discovers the money, he claims he got it from a lost wallet. This fib gets Fred into big trouble when Wilma posts an ad for the wallet's "owner."

Note: Daws Butler does the voice for Barney.

38 "Social Climbers" Airdate: November 17, 1961

When the wives get invited to a posh social event, the husbands go to charm school so they can make a good impression at the event.

39 "The Beauty Contest" Airdate: December 1, 1961

Fred and Barney don't enjoy judging for the Water Buffalo beauty contest. Not only do they fear their wives' wrath but they are pressured by certain people, including Fred's boss, to rig the contest.

40 "The Masquerade Ball" Airdate: December 8, 1961

When Fred attends a costume ball, he mistakes his boss for another guest.

41 "The Picnic" Airdate: December 15, 1961

Barney is upset because Fred chooses Joe Rockhead instead of him as his partner at the lodge picnic.

42 "The House Guest" Airdate: December 22, 1961

When their house is flooded, the Rubbles move in with the Flintstones.

But Barney is such a pain in the neck that he gets on Fred's nerves, resulting in fighting between the men.

43 "The X-Ray Story" Airdate: December 29, 1961

A mix up of Dino's and Fred's x-rays make Wilma and the Rubbles think Fred has caught dinopetitis, Dino's disease. They treat Fred by making him stay awake for 72 straight hours.

44 "The Gambler" Airdate: January 5, 1962

The gambler is Fred and his addiction results in the loss of his furniture and television to Arnold the paperboy.

45 "A Star is Almost Born" Airdate: January 12, 1962

A TV producer hires Wilma for an acting job and Fred decides to become her manager.

46 "The Entertainer" Airdate: January 19, 1962

Fred's boss compels him to entertain a female client named Greta Gravel while Wilma is away. When he takes her to a restaurant, Greta runs into Wilma and Fred fears his wife will jump to the wrong conclusions.

47 "Wilma's Vanishing Money" Airdate: January 26, 1962

Anxious to buy a bowling ball, Fred steals Wilma's money. He discovers that she intended to use the money to buy the ball as a birthday gift for her husband.

48 "Feudin' and Fussin'" Airdate: February 2, 1962

Fred and Barney are fighting again and the mutual antagonism is so strong that Barney plans to move away.

49"Impractical Joker" Airdate: February 9, 1962

Fred enjoys playing practical jokes on Barney. Barney resents being the butt of the jokes so he tries to get even by hoodwinking Fred into believing he's engaged in counterfeiting.

50"Operation Barney" Airdate: February 16, 1962

The men want to skip work to see a ball game but Barney has to report to his company's nurse. With Fred's help, Barney convinces the nurse he is too sick to work but he winds up in the hospital. Now Fred has to get Barney out without raising any suspicions.

51"The Happy Household" Airdate: February 23, 1962

Wilma is hired as host of the TV cooking show "The Happy Housewife" but Fred is unhappy because she's no longer at home to bake meals for him.

52"Fred Strikes Out" Airdate: March 2, 1962

On the anniversary of Wilma accepting Fred's marriage proposal, Fred plans to participate in a bowling match. Unwilling to miss the match but afraid of disappointing his wife, he tries to take her out and still make the tournament on the same night.

53"This is Your Lifesaver" Airdate: March 9, 1962

When Fred and Barney stop a man named J. Montague Gypsum from jumping off a bridge, he vows to be their servant for life. But he's actually a con artist who takes advantage of the men.

54"Trouble-in-Law" Airdate: March 16, 1962

Fred's mother-in-law shows up and has no intention of leaving soon.

Determined to get her out of the house, Fred tries to fix her up with a suitor.

Note: This is a direct continuation of "This is Your Lifesaver." Verna Felton does the voice of Wilma's mother.

55 "The Mailman Cometh" Airdate: March 23, 1962

Thinking that his boss, Mr. Slate, has passed him over for an annual raise, Fred mails him a nasty letter. When Fred learns that Mr. Slate made an honest mistake and is giving him a raise, he tries to retrieve the letter so he can avoid trouble with his boss.

56 "The Rock Vegas Story" Airdate: March 30, 1962

Fred meets an old school friend, Sherman, at an automat. Sherman now runs a Rock Vegas hotel and he invites the Flintstones and the Rubbles to visit. When they arrive in the city, Fred blows all of their money on a slot machine. Sherman lets them stay at the hotel but they have to work off their charges there.

57 "Divided We Sail" Airdate: April 6, 1962

Fred is supposed to be a contestant on the TV game show *The Prize is Priced* (a spoof of *The Price is Right*), but he develops stage fright and doesn't appear on the show. Barney takes his place and wins a houseboat. The husbands battle over custody of the prize.

58 "Kleptomaniac Caper" Airdate: April 13, 1962

Fred finds a box of his old clothes in Barney's car. Unaware that Wilma placed the box there (she plans to donate them to a rummage sale), he thinks Barney is stealing them.

59"Latin Lover" Airdate: April 20, 1962

Wilma becomes infatuated with the Italian actor Roberto Rockellini. Feeling slighted, Fred woos Wilma by aping Roberto's appearance mannerisms, including a moustache, ascot, and Continental charm. But Wilma worries that the "new" Fred is attracting other women and wants the "old" Fred back.

60"Take Me Out of the Ball Game" Airdate: April 27, 1962

A baseball scout is interested in hiring Fred when he sees him umpiring a Little League game.

Season 3 (1962-63)

61 Dino Goes Hollyrock" Airdate: September 14, 1962

Dino falls in love with Sassie, a lady dinosaur who stars in her own TV show. When Fred learns that the studio is looking for a male dinosaur to play opposite Sassie, he brings Dino there to audition.

Note: Sassie spoofs the popular TV dog star Lassie.

62"Fred's New Boss" Airdate: September 21, 1962

When Barney loses his job, Fred gets him hired at the quarry where he works. Barney is quickly promoted to Fred's supervisor, and Fred envies his friend's good fortune.

Note: This is the final episode where "Rise and Shine" is used in the beginning and end credits as the theme song.

63"Barney the Invisible" Airdate: September 28, 1962

Fred creates a potion to get rid of Barney's hiccups. It does make the hiccups disappear, but it also makes Barney disappear.

Note: This is the first episode where "Meet the Flintstones" is used in the beginning and end credits as the theme song.

64"Bowling Ballet" Airdate: October 5, 1962

Fred's bowling skills aren't up to par for an upcoming tournament so in order to improve them, he takes up ballet.

65"The Twitch" Airdate: October 12, 1962

Fred assures Wilma he can get a big star to perform at her upcoming benefit. He's able to persuade singing star "Rock Roll" to appear. Unfortunately, on the night of the benefit, Rock develops laryngitis. So Fred has to dress up like Rock and lip synch to his record.

66"Here's Snow in Your Eyes" Airdate: October 19, 1962

When Fred and Barney go with their lodge to a snow resort, then run into a group of jewel thieves.

67"The Buffalo Convention" Airdate: October 26, 1962

Fred gives Wilma a dodo bird for her birthday. This dodo bird can talk but he can't keep a secret- he reveals to Wilma and Betty that the men are going to a lodge convention in Frantic City- without the wives.

68"The Little Stranger" Airdate: November 2, 1962

When Fred overhears Wilma on the phone mention taking in a "little visitor", he thinks is wife is expecting a baby. But the "little visitor" is actually Arnold the paperboy.

69"Baby Barney" Airdate: November 9, 1962

Fred wants to inherit his wealthy Uncle Tex's fortune, but in order to get it he has to have a son. When Uncle Tex visits the Flintstones, Barney poses as Fred and Wilma's child.

70 "Hawaiian Escapade" Airdate: November 16, 1962

Wilma and Betty win a contest for an all-expenses trip to Hawaii. When the husbands and wives arrive there, Fred is hired as stunt double for star Larry Lava on the TV show *Hawaiian Spy* (a spoof of *Hawaiian Eye*).

71 "Ladies' Day" Airdate: November 23, 1962

"Ladies Day" is when women can see a baseball game for free. Eager to see the game that day but short of cash, Fred disguises himself as a lady.

72 "Nuttin' but the Tooth" Airdate: November 30, 1962

Fred wants to see a boxing match but Barney comes down with a toothache. In order to save money so he can see the fight, Fred takes his friend to a veterinary dentist, who is cheaper than a dentist for people. But Barney is given too much anesthetic gas and flies out of the dentist's office.

73 "High School Fred" Airdate: December 7, 1962

Fred returns to high school to complete his studies so he doesn't lose his job. Even though he is older than the other students, he becomes very popular at school.

74 "Dial 'S' for Suspicion" Airdate: December 14, 1962

Wilma is reading a novel about a woman who kills her husband. Meanwhile, Fred experiences a series of accidents and he fears that his wife is trying to bump him off so she can collect life insurance money.

75 "Flash Gun Freddie" Airdate: December 21, 1962

Fred and Barney go into the photography business and inadvertently take a picture of two fleeing bank robbers.

Note: "Flash gun" refers to a flashgun, a flash device for a camera that could be used for indoor photography at a time when film was less light-sensitive.

76 "The Kissing Burglar" Airdate: January 4, 1963

Wilma is infatuated by an amorous burglar who is roaming Bedrock.

77 "Wilma, the Maid" Airdate: January 11, 1963

Fred hires a maid, Lollobrickida, but she quits because she can't stand his singing. Meanwhile, Fred has invited his boss to dinner and has told him about the maid. In order to keep in the boss's good graces, Wilma pretends to be the maid.

78 "The Hero" Airdate: January 18, 1963

Barney rescues a baby but Fred is hailed as a hero in the press. Fred's ghostly conscience torments him for stealing the credit for Barney's gallantry.

79 "The Surprise" Airdate: January 25, 1963

Fred's in a dither because he believes Barney is too occupied with his baby nephew Marblehead to spend time with him. He claims that he hates babies but when Wilma tells him she's expecting a child, Fred is overjoyed.

80 "Mother-In-Law's Visit" Airdate: February 1, 1963

Fred is unhappy that his mother-in-law is staying at his house to help Wilma prepare for the new baby. Needing money to get a crib, he takes a job as a taxi driver. Wearing a disguise, he's able to make the money driving his mother-in-law all over town.

81 "Foxy Grandma" Airdate: February 8, 1963

When Fred's mother-in-law leaves, he hires a housekeeper to help the expecting Wilma. Unfortunately, she happens to be a notorious bank robber.

82 "Fred's New Job" Airdate: February 15, 1963

Aware of the expenses of having a new baby, Fred tries to get a raise from Mr. Slate but winds up getting fired. Fred messes up each successive job he takes. Finally, Mr. Slate rehires him and gives him a big raise.

83 "Dress Rehearsal" Airdate: February 22, 1963

Fred and Wilma become the proud parents of a girl named Pebbles but before the blessed event, Fred undergoes a series of mishaps when trying to take Wilma to the hospital.

84 "Carry On, Nurse Fred" Airdate: March 1, 1963

Frustrated with the nurse that his mother-in-law has sent to help Wilma care for Pebbles, Fred fires her and unsuccessfully tries to fulfill her duties.

85 "Ventriloquist Barney" Airdate: March 8, 1963

Using his ventriloquism skills, Barney fools Fred into thinking Pebbles can talk. When Fred gets wise, he's enraged with Barney. He then makes up with him and the two men decide to go to a wrestling match. Fred hires a babysitter to look after Pebbles but instead of doing her job, she holds a party. Fred and Barney wind up taking the baby to the wrestling tournament.

86 "The Big Move" Airdate: March 22, 1963

Worried that Pebbles is growing up in a low class environment, Fred moves the family to a posh neighborhood. He soon regrets that decision and decides his daughter's better off in the old neighborhood.

87 "Swedish Visitors" Airdate: March 29, 1963

The Flintstones go on a camping trip. When Fred drives his sleeping wife and daughter home, he discovers some Swedish musicians in his house. Fred learns that Wilma has rented the house to them so she can get back the money she has borrowed from a bank account.

Note: Yogi Bear and Boo Boo, a regular on Yogi's show, make cameos.

88 "The Birthday Party" Airdate: April 5, 1963

Wilma plans a surprise birthday party for Fred. Barney keeps Fred away from the house until the party is ready by driving him around town, but things go haywire for the husbands.

Note: Although this was the last episode aired in the third season, it was made before Wilma announced her pregnancy, so Pebbles does not appear.

Season 4 (1963-64)

89 "Ann-Margrock Presents" Airdate: September 19, 1963

The singing star Ann-Margrock (voiced by special guest star Ann-Margret) arrives in Bedrock for a show. When she gets a flat tire, she stays with the Flintstones, but they don't recognize her. Meanwhile, Fred and Barney want to perform with Ann-Margrock at the Bedrock Bowl. She gives them the opportunity and they eventually find out her real identity.

90 "Groom Gloom" Airdate: September 26, 1963

Arnold the paper boy enjoys playing with Pebbles but when he joshes that someday he'll marry her, Fred is not amused. (Previous episodes like "The Gambler" reveal the boy has been a thorn in Fred's side.) Fred has a nightmare about a future where an adult Arnold takes over his job and elopes with a teenaged Pebbles.

Note: Janet Waldo does the voice of the teenaged Pebbles.

91 "Little Bamm-Bamm" Airdate: October 3, 1963

The Rubbles envy the Flintstones being parents and they wish on a falling star for a child of their own. They get their wish when they find a baby boy in a basket on their door step. A note in the basket reveals his name is Bamm Bamm and he displays exceptional physical strength. Barney and Betty want to adopt him, but they get into a custody battle with a wealthy man who also wants to adopt him.

Note: Although this episode was the third episode to be aired in the fourth season, it was actually produced later than the nine following aired episodes in which Bamm Bamm is absent.

92 "Dino Disappears" Airdate: October 10, 1963

When Fred forgets Dino's birthday and wrongly accuses him of trying to harm Pebbles, the disconsolate dinosaur runs away. Fred and Barney look for him and mistake a stunt/dancing animal named "Rocky" for him. Fred swears he'll spend one week in Dino's dog house if he got the wrong dinosaur. When Dino is reunited with the Flintstones, Fred unhappily does just that.

93 "Fred's Monkeyshines" Airdate: October 17, 1963

Fred needs glasses but he gets the wrong pair and not only does have trouble seeing, he thinks a circus monkey is Pebbles.

94 "The Flintstone Canaries" Airdate: October 24, 1963

Fred and Barney form a barbershop quartet so they can audition on the popular TV show *Hum Along with Herman*. Barney can sing beautifully, but only when he's in the bathtub.

Note: *Hum Along with Herman* is a lampoon of the then popular NBC show *Sing Along with Mitch*.

95 "Glue for Two" Airdate: October 31, 1963

Fred invents a strong superglue. It proves to be too strong because he and Barney get stuck together on Barney's new bowling ball.

96 "Big League Freddie" Airdate: November 7, 1963

When Fred hurts himself while trying out for a Major League baseball team, his friend Roger Marble dons Fred's uniform and fills in for him. Major-league scouts see Roger play and sign him up, mistaking him for Fred.

97 "Old Lady Betty" Airdate: November 14, 1963

Betty wants to buy Barney a rocking chair. Masquerading as an old lady, she gets a job running errands for a wheelchair-bound old woman. But the seemingly frail woman is actually a young and spry counterfeiter named Greta Gravel in disguise and she is using Betty as an unwitting pawn in her dirty work.

98"Sleep On, Sweet Fred" Airdate: November 21, 1963

Feeling that Fred and Barney don't give them enough respect, Wilma and
Betty hypnotize their sleeping husbands to make them not only treat
them better but to get them nice presents. The husbands eventually
get wise to the wives' scheme. Fred and Barney try to turn the tables
on Wilma and Betty by pretending to plan to get them mink coats
through illegal means.

99"Kleptomaniac Pebbles" Airdate: November 28, 1963

A crook named Baffles Gravel plants a stolen necklace in Pebbles' carriage.
When Fred discovers the necklace, he fears that his daughter will grow
up to be a kleptomaniac.

Note: Betty does not appear in this episode.

100"Daddy's Little Beauty" Airdate: December 5, 1963

Fred enters Pebbles in a beauty contest. He thinks the contest is for babies
but it's actually for young women.

101"Daddies Anonymous" Airdate: December 12, 1963

Fred and Barney take Pebbles and Bamm Bamm for strolls so they don't
have to do weekend housework. The men discover a club where they
can park the babies in their carriages and play cards and have fun with
the other fathers.

102"Peek-a-Boo Camera" Airdate: December 19, 1963

In order to attend a bachelor party without arousing the wives' suspicions,
Fred and Barney tell Wilma and Betty that they are paying their last
respects for a dying friend. The husbands enjoy themselves at the party
but they panic when they learn it has been secretly televised for the

popular TV show *Peek-a-Boo Camera*. Fred and Barney desperately try to prevent their wives from seeing them on the show.

Note: *Peek-a-Boo Camera* is a spoof of *Candid Camera*.

103 "Once Upon a Coward" Airdate: December 26, 1963

When Fred gives to a mugger's demands, he feels like a coward. Determined to salvage his pride, Fred plans to catch the mugger.

104 "Ten Little Flintstones" Airdate: January 2, 1964

When ten robots who look like Fred come to earth from outer space, they commit all kinds of mayhem and Fred gets the blame.

105: "Fred El Terrifico" Airdate: January 9, 1964

The Flintsones and the Rubbles vacation in Rockapulco, Mexico. Getting into the spirit of the trip, Fred grows a mustache and poses as a secret agent called El Terrifico. But two jewel thieves try to use him as a patsy in their smuggling scheme.

Note: Janet Waldo replaces Verna Felton as the voice of Wilma's mother.

106 "The Bedrock Hillbillies" Airdate: January 16, 1964

When Fred inherits an estate, he takes his family to the place to claim it but he stumbles upon a long-running feud between the Flintstones and the Hatrocks.

Note: The title is a play on the hit sitcom *The Beverly Hillbillies*.

107 "Flintstone and the Lion" Airdate: January 23, 1964

The lion is a cub Fred discovers on a fishing trip. Thinking he's a kitten, he brings him home but the cub matures into a big, hungry lion. If

Fred doesn't get rid of him, the beast will inadvertently wreck the Flintstones' home.

108"Cave Scout Jamboree" Airdate: January 30, 1964

When a flood at his job causes Fred to be laid off for a week, he tries to take advantage of his time off by taking his family and the Rubbles camping. If they're hoping a restful time, they won't get it because cave scouts from all over the world are holding a jamboree where the Flintstones and Rubbles stay.

109"Room for Two" Airdate: February 6, 1964

When Barney doesn't vote for Fred as Grand Poobah of their lodge, Fred declares he wants nothing to do with Barney. But he can't get rid of his ex-friend because a newly built room in Fred's house is on half of Barney's property.

110"Ladies' Night at the Lodge" Airdate: February 13, 1964

Masquerading as men, Wilma and Betty sneak into Fred and Barney's lodge to find out what their husbands do there.

111"Reel Trouble" Airdate: February 20, 1964

Fred annoys Wilma and his friends with his home movies of Pebbles's trivial activities. His passion accidentally gets him mixed up with some crooks.

112"Son of Rockzilla" Airdate: February 27, 1964

Fred is hired by a Hollyrock film company to play the monster in their production *Son of Rockzilla*. Unfortunately, once filming ends, he can't get his mask off and winds up being chased by both the police and a lovesick creature that has escaped the zoo.

113"Bachelor Daze" Airdate: March 5, 1964

When the Flintstones and the Rubbles learn that the Honeyrock Hotel is going to be torn down to make room for a supermarket, they reminisce about the place where they first met.

114"Operation Switchover" Airdate: March 12, 1964

The switchover is between Fred and Wilma in their roles. Each one thinks the other has it easier so Fred becomes a househusband while Wilma takes over Fred's job for one day.

Note: Bea Benaderet voices Betty Rubble for the last time in this episode.

Season 5 (1964-65)

115"Hop Happy" Airdate: September 17, 1964

Barney and Betty get a new pet, a prehistoric kangaroo named Hoppy. Fred is not pleased with the new addition to the Rubble family.

Note: Gerry Johnson replaces Bea Benaderet as Betty Rubble in this episode.

116"Monster Fred" Airdate: September 24, 1964

A blow on the head with a bowling ball makes Fred act like a little boy. Barney thinks Dr. Frankenstone is the right specialist to help his friend but he's actually a mad scientist experimenting with mind switching.

117   "Itty Bitty Fred" Airdate: October 1, 1964

Fred creates a weight reducing concoction called "Fred-O-Cal." The concoction causes Fred to lose more weight than he expects- it makes him less than a foot tall.

118 "Pebbles' Birthday Party" Airdate: October 8, 1964

On the same night Pebbles will have her first birthday party and Fred's lodge will have its own party. But the caterer goofs up, dispatching dancing girls to the Flintstones' house and a clown to the lodge.

119 "Bedrock Rodeo Round-Up" Airdate: October 15, 1964

Fred is envious of Wilma's old beau Bony Hurdle when he wows her and Pebbles with his rodeo tricks so he tries to top him by entering the Bedrock Rodeo.

120 "Cinderellastone" Airdate: October 22, 1964

Mr. Slate invites all his employees to his house party except Fred. Feeling peeved, Fred dreams he has a fairy godmother who uses her powers to make him a well-dressed gentleman and bring him to the party.

121 "A Haunted House is Not a Home" Airdate: October 29, 1964

Fred's Uncle Giggles plays an elaborate practical joke on his nephew. Pretending to be dead, he leaves his fortune to Fred, providing he stay overnight at his haunted house.

122 "Dr. Sinister" Airdate: November 5, 1964

Fred and Barney go on an errand to the store for their wives. They wind up kidnapped and flown to a volcanic island where they encounter the diabolical scientist Dr. Sinister.

Note: This episode lampoons the James Bond film *Dr. No.*

123 "The Gruesomes" Airdate: November 12, 1964

The Gruesome family's eerie behavior doesn't endear them to their new neighbor Fred.

Notes: The Gruesomes spoofed two live-action horror sitcoms on the air at this time- *The Addams Family* and *The Munsters*, the latter running opposite *The Flintstones*.

124 "The Most Beautiful Baby in Bedrock" Airdate: November 19, 1964

Fred and Barney's friendship turns to mutual antagonism when both men enter their children in a beauty contest for babies.

125 "Dino and Juliet" Airdate: November 26, 1964

Dino falls in love with the female dinosaur next door. The problem is that her owner, Mr. Loudrock, doesn't get along with Fred.

126 "King for a Night" Airdate: December 3, 1964

While visiting Bedrock, the King of Stonesylvania gets fed up with the royal protocol and skedaddles to enjoy the freedom of the common people. The King's frantic attendants spot Fred, notice he looks exactly like the missing monarch, and persuade him to appear at public ceremonies. Both Fred and the King are frustrated with their new situations and eventually and gratefully return to their normal roles.

Note: This episode revamps the first season episode, "The Tycoon".

127 "Indianrockolis 500" Airdate: December 10, 1964

Fred and Barney enter the racing tournament Indianrockolis 500, planning to use the prize money for their children's education. But they have trouble handling their car.

128 "Adobe Dick" Airdate: December 17, 1964

Fred and Barney go fishing but wind up being swallowed by a whale called Adobe Dick.

129"Christmas Flintstone" Airdate: December 25, 1964

In order to raise money to buy Christmas presents for his family and friends, Fred gets a job playing Santa Claus at Macyrock's (a parody of Macy's). Meanwhile, the real Santa Claus is too sick to deliver gifts on Christmas Eve so his elves get Fred to take his place.

130"Fred's Flying Lesson" Airdate: January 1, 1965

When Fred wins a flying lesson at a lodge raffle, he dreams of becoming a professional pilot.

131"Fred's Second Car" Airdate: January 8, 1965

Fred thinks he's has it made when he purchases a car for virtually nothing from a police auction. But the car belongs to gangsters and when Fred and Barney go for a ride in it, they finds themselves menaced by them.

132"Time Machine" Airdate: January 15, 1965

When the Flintstones and Rubbles go to the Bedrock World's Fair, they see a time machine in a science exhibit. The time machine actually works and the husbands and wives find themselves in various periods in the future.

133"The Hatrocks and the Gruesomes" Airdate: January 22, 1965

Declaring the feud is over, the Hatrocks show up at the Flintstones' house. But the visitors prove to be freeloading pests. The Flintstones then learn that the Hatrocks can't stand "bug music" (a lampoon of the Beatles). With the help of the Rubbles and the Gruesomes, they drive the Hatrocks away by playing and singing the "bug music" hit "She Said Yeah Yeah Yeah" (a takeoff of the Beatles' smash "She Loves You").

Note: The Hatrocks and Gruesomes both make their second and final appearances on the show.

134"Moonlight and Maintenance" Airdate: January 29, 1965

Fred decides to move his family to a posh apartment. But when he does, he moonlights as the apartment complex's custodian so he can pay for the place. The workload for his new job interferes with his duties for his old job at the gravel pits.

135"Sheriff for a Day" Airdate: February 5, 1965

Taking a vacation in the western desert, the Flintstones and the Rubbles visit a ghost town. The Sheriff happens to be an old chum of Fred's and he appoints him sheriff for a day. What Fred doesn't know is that some outlaws plan to shoot whoever is sheriff on that day.

Note: This was the only episode to air without a laugh track, but a later syndicated print was given one.

136"Deep in the Heart of Texarock" Airdate: February 12, 1965

Fred's Uncle Tex invites the Flintstones and the Rubbles to his ranch in Texarock. There, Fred and Barney try to foil cow rustlers.

137"The Rolls Rock Caper" Airdate: February 19, 1965

A detective named Aaron Boulder recruits the husbands to help in stop criminals. Fred and Barney learn they're actually guest stars on a TV show called *Smile, You're on My Favorite Crime*.

Note: "Aaron Boulder" is a spoof of Gene Barry's "Amos Burke", the lead character in the TV show *Burke's Law*.

138"Superstone" Airdate: February 26, 1965

Fred gets a new job playing the TV hero "Superstone." But two crooks frame him for a robbery.

139"Fred Meets Hercurock" Airdate: March 5, 1965

Fred gets another new job- the heroic title role in the movie *Hercurock*. But Fred learns that film stardom has its drawbacks.

140"Surfin' Fred" Airdate: March 12, 1965

The Flintstones and Rubbles go on another vacation to Rock Island. There a surfing tournament judged by the singing star Jimmy Darrock (special guest star James Darren) is being held. Even though Fred has never surfed in his life, he participates in the contest over Wilma's objections.

Note: This episode's soundtrack   plugs two songs from the Fantastic Baggys' 1964 album *Tell 'Em I'm Surfin'*- "Wax Up Your Board" and "Surfin' Craze".

Season 6 (1965-66)

141"No Biz Like Show Biz" Airdate: September 17, 1965

Fred dreams that Pebbles and Bamm Bamm can sing and play music and become pop stars under the guidance of talent scout Eppy Brianstone.

Notes: Eppy Brianstone is a takeoff of Beatles manager Brian Epstein. Pebbles and Bamm Bamm perform a song "Open Up Your Heart (And Let the Sunshine In)" which is reprised in the show's closing credits.

142"The House that Fred Built" Airdate: September 24, 1965

The Flintstones receive a letter from Fred's mother-in-law stating she plans to move in with her favorite son-in-law and wife. Fred isn't happy about the idea of living with his mother-in-law so he with Barney's assistance, he tries to fix up an old house for her to stay in.

143"The Return of Stony Curtis" Airdate: October 1, 1965

Promoting his upcoming film *Slave Boy*, Stony Curtis (voiced by special guest star Tony Curtis) promises for a day to be slave for whoever wins a contest. Wilma, who idolizes Curtis, is the lucky winner.

144"Disorder in the Court" Airdate: October 8, 1965

Fred and Barney do jury duty, with Fred as foreman. Fred makes the decision to convict "The Mangler" of robbery. The sentenced criminal threatens retribution against Fred and when he escapes from jail, Fred worries that the Mangler will carry out his revenge.

145"Circus Business" Airdate: October 15, 1965

When the Flintstones and the Rubbles visit a circus, Fred purchases it. But the circus performers walk out on him because they haven't been paid and Fred doesn't have enough money to pay them. Fred and Barney try to put on a show themselves to attract customers.

146"Samantha" Airdate: October 22, 1965

Elizabeth Montgomery and Dick York guest star as animated versions of their *Bewitched* characters Samantha and Darrin who move in next door to the Flintstones. The husbands go on a camping trip alone. The wives resent being left home so they go on their own trip with Samantha. Samantha uses her magical powers so everything goes right on their vacation.

Note: Hanna-Barbera was responsible for the TV show *Bewitched*'s opening animated title sequence.

147 "The Great Gazoo" Airdate: October 29, 1965

An extraterrestrial named Gazoo from the planet Zetox is sent to Earth to study the behavior of its inhabitants. He meets Fred and Barney and astounds them with his magical abilities. Gazoo promises to use them to give the husbands money so they can take their wives to a costly restaurant. But Gazoo doesn't show up with the money when the Flintstones and Rubbles get the bill so Fred and Barney wind up washing dishes in the restaurant.

148 "Rip Van Flintstone" Airdate: November 5, 1965

Fred falls asleep at a company picnic and dreams of waking up after 20 years. A lot has changed- his friends are no longer around, Barney is wealthy, and Pebbles and Bamm Bamm are husband and wife. He is distressed that he has let so much time pass by, but Fred is relieved to wake up and learn he only slept for an hour.

Note: Gazoo does not appear in this episode.

149 "The Gravelberry Pie King" Airdate: November 12, 1965

When Mr. Slate fires Fred for demanding a raise for himself and the other workers (the other workers get their raise), he goes to work for P.J. Safestone of Safestone Supermarkets (a spoof of Safeway Supermarkets). Fred tries to supply Safestone with his wife's homemade gravelberry pies but his efforts to sell them are less than successful.

Note: Gazoo appears in this episode.

150 "The Stonefinger Caper" Airdate: November 19, 1965

A secret organization planning to take over the world want to abduct the brilliant scientist Dr. Rockenheimer because he has a formula that will enable them to attain their goal. But they mistake Barney for the scientist.

Note: Gazoo appears in this episode.

151 "The Masquerade Party" Airdate: November 26, 1965

Fred goes to a masquerade party dressed as an extraterrestrial. Unfortunately for him, on the night of the party, , a radio station pulls a prank that aliens called the Way-Outs are invading thing and Fred is mistaken for one of them.

Note: Gazoo does not appear in this episode.

152 "Shinrock-A-Go-Go" Airdate: December 3, 1965

When Fred yells and hops in pain after a bowling ball falls on his foot, he inadvertently creates a new dance craze, "the frantic".

Note: *Shinrock* is a spoof of the popular teen variety show *Shindig*. The show's host Jimmy O'Neill guest voices as "Jimmy O'Neillstone". The rock group the Beau Brummels also do guest voicework as "The Beau Brummelstones". Gazoo does not appear in this episode.

153 "Royal Rubble" Airdate: December 10, 1965

A royal tribe spots Barney and mistake him for their missing prince.

Note: "Open Your Heart" is used for the second time over the closing credits. Gazoo does not appear in this episode.

154"Seeing Doubles" Airdate: December 17, 1965

How can Fred and Barney take their wives to dinner and still go to the bowling game the same night? Gazoo devises two doubles of the husbands to take the wives out. But these doubles get Fred and Barney into hot water.

155"How to Pick a Fight with Your Wife Without Really Trying" Airdate: January 7, 1966

Gazoo acts as Fred's marriage counselor, telling him his relationship with Wilma could be improved by a Monopoly game. But this game results in a marital quarrel and they temporarily split up.

156"Fred Goes Ape" Airdate: January 14, 1966

Fred suffers from allergies so for treatment he takes medicine pills called "Scram." But these pills make him turn into an ape.

Note: "Open Your Heart" is used for the last time over the closing credits. Gazoo does not appear in this episode.

157"The Long, Long, Long Weekend" Airdate: January 21, 1966

Needing some money to fix up his backyard for the weekend, Fred borrows four dollars from Mr. Slate. He plans to spend the entire weekend in the backyard with his family and the Rubbles. Instead, Fred, Wilma, Barney and Betty travel into the 21st century, courtesy of Gazoo. There, Fred meets a descendant of Mr. Slate and discovers that he's still in debt for the loan, plus millions of dollars in interest.

Note: Since the 21st century setting is the same as for *The Jetsons*, the music score from the canceled series is used.

158"Two Men on a Dinosaur" Airdate: February 4, 1966

Fred and Barney win money at a dinosaur race track, thanks to the Great Gazoo's magical intervention. But some gangsters take advantage of their lucky streak by abducting them so Fred and Barney can make money for them.

159"The Treasure of Sierra Madrock" Airdate: February 11, 1966

On their way back from Rock Vegas, Fred and Barney encounter two swindlers posing as gold miners. The swindlers sell the men a phony gold mine.

Note: Gazoo does not appear in this episode.

160"Curtain Call at Bedrock" Airdate: February 18, 1966

The Flintstones and the Rubbles try to stage the play *Romeorock and Julietstone*. Fred is cast as Romeorock and Wilma as Julietstone. When Wilma gets laryngitis on opening night, Barney fills in.

Note: Gazoo appears in this episode.

161"Boss for a Day" Airdate: February 25, 1966

The boss for a day is Fred, thanks to Gazoo's powers. But after a hard day trying to run the business, Fred decides he's better off as a lowly employee.

162"Fred's Island" Airdate: March 4, 1966

Mr. Slate has a yacht and he orders Fred to paint. Barney helps out, but the yacht drifts away to what the husbands think is an uncharted island.

Note: The title is a play on the TV sitcom *Gilligan's Island*. Gazoo does not appear in this episode.

163 "Jealousy" Airdate: March 11, 1966

Fred decides to go bowling rather than go to the ball with Wilma. Determined to go to the ball with an escort, Wilma chooses a old boyfriend to escort her. A jealous Fred plans to crash the party with his own escort. The escort is Barney, who thanks to Gazoo, becomes a lovely woman named Barbara.

Note: Betty, Pebbles, Bamm-Bamm and Dino don't appear in this episode.

164 "Dripper" Airdate: March 18, 1966

When the Flintstones go to an aquarium to see Dripper the sealasuarus (a spoof on the TV show *Flipper* about a dolphin) perform, the animal follows them home. Two crooks try to abduct Dripper but they kidnap Barney instead.

Note: Gazoo does not appear in this episode.

165 "My Fair Freddy" Airdate: March 25, 1966

The Flintstones are invited to a swanky party and Fred worries that he doesn't know the proper decorum. So Gazoo tries to make Fred more refined by giving him ballet lessons.

Note: The Great Gazoo makes his final appearance in this episode.

166 "The Story of Rocky's Raiders" Airdate: April 1, 1966

Discovered in a crate is the diary of Fred's grandfather Rocky Flintstone. This diary details Rocky's military exploits during Stone World War I.

Top Cat

Broadcast Station: ABC. Telecast: September 27, 1961-September 26, 1962. Studio: Hanna-Barbera/Screen Gems. Produced and directed by William Hanna and Joseph Barbera. Associate producer, Alan Dinehart. Production supervisor, Howard Hanson. Backgrounds by Fernando Montealegre. Music by Hoyt Curtin. Theme song by Hanna and Barbera. Animation director: Charles A. Nichols. Animation by Kenneth Muse and Jerry Hathcock. Voices: Arnold Stang (Top Cat); Allen Jenkins (Officer Dibble); Maurice Gosfield (Benny the Ball); Marvin Kaplan (Choo Choo); Leo de Lyon (Spook/The Brain); John Stephenson (Fancy Fancy); and Daws Butler, Don Messick, Paul Frees, Jean Vander Pyl, Bea Benaderet, and GeGe Pearson, among others.

The Phil Silvers Show centered on the schemes of Master Sergeant Ernie Bilko (Silvers) to upgrade his austere living standards, outsmarting his superiors, particularly Colonel John Hall (Paul Ford). His motley platoon of enlisted men aided Bilko. As an animated version of Bilko, Top Cat would be an alley cat using his wits to obtain material comforts, hoodwinking Officer Dibble, a human cop on the beat in Top Cat's alley. Just as Bilko had his platoon to help him carry out his plans, Top Cat would have a gang of other alley cats to help him carry out *his*.

Growing up in New York City, Joe Barbera could personally relate to *Top Cat*'s street con artist concept. He didn't grow up in an alley and his family never had to scrounge for food, but Barbera's environment "was a place that demanded all your wit to survive, let alone get ahead. It helped if you were the kind of smart aleck who knew all the angles and whose smooth-talking charm would you give you the force of personality that made you top cat."

Another significant influence on *Top Cat* was the low-budget Bowery Boys comedies in the 1940s and 1950s. Produced by Monogram (which evolved into Allied Artists while the films were being made), this series centered on a group of New York City hooligans who talked tough but had hearts of gold. Like Bilko's platoon, the Bowery Boys had a conniving, streetwise leader, the malaprop-spouting Slip Mahoney (Leo Gorcey). And the Boys themselves were a ragtag bunch, particularly the enthusiastic but dimwitted Sach Jones (Huntz Hall). Just as Bilko's soldiers took advantage of Colonel Hall, the Bowery Boys took advantage of Louie Dumbrowski (Bernard Gorcey, Leo's father), the proprietor of a candy store called Louie's Sweet Shop.

Yet another antecedent was an earlier Hanna-Barbera character, Yogi Bear. Originally, the bear's show was a segment of *The Huckleberry Hound Show* but Yogi became so popular that in 1961, just before *Top Cat* premiered, he headlined his own program, *The Yogi Bear Show*. A denizen of Jellystone Park, the rascally creature constantly irked the human park ranger John Smith with his schemes to poach tourists' picnic baskets. Just as Top Cat would resemble Yogi Bear, Officer Dibble would resemble Ranger Smith.

(Bill and Joe's rehashing of an earlier cartoon's format for *Top Cat* was a harbinger for a gradual decline in Hanna-Barbera's creativity. As the cartoon studio expanded and produced more programs, Bill and Joe began to spread themselves too thin. Hanna-Barbera's staff were under so much pressure to complete the programs on time and on budget that there was little room for innovation or inspiration. When Bill and Joe started producing cartoons for Saturday morning, they were further stifled by meddling network executives obsessed with ratings but unconcerned about quality. By the end of the 1960s, Hanna-Barbera had fallen into an artistic rut.)

Top Cat was not Bill and Joe's first choice for the name of their new conniving cat; they wanted to call him *Tomcat*. But that name sounded too similar to their earlier cat Tom of the cinematic team of Tom and Jerry. And in an era when the Federal Communications Commission's (FCC's) censorship standards were far stricter than they are today, Hanna-Barbera worried that Tomcat sounded too suggestive. *Top Cat* was both inoffensive and original. (Ironically, when *Top Cat* was broadcast in Great Britain, the title had to be changed to *Boss Cat* because at the time, there was a commercial cat food with that name in the United Kingdom.)

Daws Butler did a brilliant Phil Silvers impersonation. But at the time of production for *Top Cat*, he was already using this voice for another Hanna-Barbera character called Hokey Wolf (who was created to support Huckleberry Hound when Yogi Bear got his own show). Besides, he was too busy with voiceovers for other television cartoons, not to mention theatrical cartoons, to be fully committed to *Top Cat*. He would only voice one episode, as a rival feline con artist trying to muscle in on Top Cat's territory.

Joe Barbera decided to cast Michael O'Shea as Top Cat's voice. O'Shea was typecast in films as a charming, easygoing man and Barbera felt that his persona, along with his slightly Brooklynese accent, would suit the citified character. But Top Cat, like Sgt. Bilko, was supposed to be a fast talker, the better to persuade his assistants and hoodwink his targets. O'Shea at his audition could not handle the dialogue's rat-a-tat pace.

Character actor Arnold Stang, who was experienced in cartoon voiceovers, auditioned for the role of Top Cat. Not only could he handle fast-paced dialogue but he had an ideal voice for the character. Joe Barbera described it as "a nasal blend of streetwise expressiveness with just a touch of the carnival barker's whine." Bill and Joe had found their Top Cat. Stang's voice also influenced the character's design. Top Cat was originally sketched to look like a pathetic bum. But Stang's voice had, in his words, "a sort of seedy grandeur, a shabby aristocracy." Top Cat's wardrobe was upgraded from a torn hat and old clothes to a straw chapeau with an Ivy League band and a colored weskit.

But Stang initially had another problem during early voiceover sessions; he sounded *too much* like Phil Silvers's Ernie Bilko. One of the sponsors warned Stang to sound more original; he was hired not because he was a good Silvers mimic but because he was a talented performer in his own right. Stang got the message and came up with a voice that sounded reminiscent of Silvers but not *exactly* like him.

On *The Phil Silvers Show*, Bilko's platoon had a short, rotund, childlike patsy named Private Duane Doberman (Maurice Gosfield). Doberman was a bungler but he looked up to Bilko as a surrogate father. Hanna-Barbera devised a Doberman-like foil for Top Cat, a diminutive, chubby feline called Benny the Ball. In order to make his resemblance to Doberman even more pronounced, the studio hired his player, Gosfield, to voice Benny. *Top Cat* would be Gosfield's only regular post-*Bilko* employment; he had trouble finding steady work because of his limited acting ability and difficulties memorizing lines. (He didn't have to memorize his lines for *Top Cat* since he read them from a script off camera.) Gosfield passed away in 1964, two years after *Top Cat*'s cancellation.

Other actors were hired to voice the rest of Top Cat's gang. These characters weren't knockoffs of *Bilko*'s supporting characters but had original personalities. As Choo Choo, Marvin Kaplan conveyed what historian Hal Erickson described as "the perfect combination of milquetoast trepidation and Manhattan street savvy". John Stephenson, already a voice actor at Hanna-Barbera (among other roles, he became a semi-regular on *The Flintstones* as Fred's boss Mr. Slate), played Fancy Fancy as a smooth-talking romancer, "the Cary Grant of Brooklyn," as he put it. Leo de Lyon did double duty as Spook, a cat with his head in the clouds who talked like a beatnik, and The Brain, who was slow witted despite his name. Allan Jenkins, who played tough guys in countless live-action Warner Brothers films during the 1930s and 1940s, was inspired casting as Officer Dibble. As hard boiled as his flesh-and-blood characters, Jenkins also gave the policeman an innate warmth beneath his bluster. Dibble had an amusing love-hate relationship with Top Cat and his gang, irritated by their shenanigans but missing them when they weren't around.

Like *The Flintstones*, *Top Cat* was promoted by Hanna-Barbera as an adult cartoon show. Bill Hanna believed that viewers of all ages would identify with Top Cat and his feline cohorts. He told the press, "Stray alley cats have real living problems with which viewers can easily identify. They're going to understand the gang's struggle for survival, and they're going to enjoy the fun they have with their freedom." Arnold Stang backed up Bill and Joe in stressing the show's universal appeal. He told reporter Richard Lake how *Top Cat* would attract both adults and children: "The dialogue appeals to the adults and the pictures appeal to the children. I think it's a very happy marriage." Stang also told Lake viewers could relate to the title character: "Top Cat is someone the viewers can easily identify with someone else they know. Maybe it's the guy down the street or their boss or even their mother-in-law."

Top Cat first aired on September 27, 1961. The critical reaction was tepid. *Variety*'s reviewer was typical of the lukewarm response: "Based on the antics of a hip-talking flock of easy-living felines, 'Top Cat' registered as a simple comic strip with no point of view to give it a cutting edge...The opening show had occasional flashes of wit, but the patter was generally a routine brand of hip jargon." The critics had also been indifferent toward *The Flintstones* when it premiered. Would *Top Cat*, like *The Flintstones*, enjoy impressive ratings to compensate for the unenthusiastic write-ups?

On the contrary- ratings were dismal. Five weeks after its premiere, one of the show's sponsors, the pharmaceutical company Bristol-Myers, wanted to end its association with *Top Cat*, although it did continue to sponsor the show for the rest of the season. But by December, Bill and Joe were expecting *Top Cat* to be cancelled. Hanna told the press that the studio was contemplating new primetime cartoons to replace the ailing show. (One new primetime cartoon was aired the following season, *The Jetsons*.)

Somehow, all thirty scheduled episodes of *Top Cat* were aired from September 1961 to April 1962. They would be the *only* episodes. In the fall of

1962, reruns were exiled to the Saturday morning's children's slot. *Top Cat* had the dubious distinction of being Hanna-Barbera's first failure on television.

Why didn't *Top Cat* attract many viewers? Hal Erickson points out that adults could not relate to the characters's shenanigans: "What grownup in 1961...could 'identify' with a gang of alley cats who tried to flummox a musical-comedy cop? *The Flintstones* appealed to adults because it mirrored adult situations; the whole 'smart animals vs. human establishment' conceit on *Top Cat* was, so far as most adults of the period were concerned, mere kid's stuff."

So why didn't many children watch *Top Cat*? The show was aired on Wednesday a half hour after another cartoon show, *The Alvin Show*, which aired on CBS. Erickson points out that parents would only allow the youngsters to watch one cartoon on a school night: " 'You've already seen your cartoon tonight,' one can hear the Moms and Dads of America saying on any Wednesday evening in early 1962. 'Now...do your homework.' " If *Top Cat* had been aired on Friday or Saturday nights, parents wouldn't have been so concerned. When reruns did turn up on Saturday mornings, they were a big hit with youngsters.

It's a shame that *Top Cat* wasn't a popular success when it was initially broadcast. Like *The Flintstones* it can be enjoyed by both children and adults. A lot of today's adult fans first got hooked on *Top Cat* when they were children. Although the show lacks *The Flintstones*'s outlandish visual gags, it is peppered with lively dialogue. The one-liners are not only bright and sassy but occasionally go over the heads of youngsters. In one episode, Top Cat's on a date with two female cats and claims he knows celebrities like Marlon Brando: "I knew him when you could understand what he was saying," a dig at Brando's trademark onscreen mumbling. The patter's sharpness is enhanced by the actors' fast paced delivery, particularly Arnold Stang as Top Cat and Allan Jenkins as Officer Dibble. The dialogue and the voice acting aren't the only contributions to *Top Cat*'s palpable urban atmosphere. Artist Fernando Montealegre adorns the backgrounds with attractive and convincing city settings. And Hoyt Curtin's score, strongly influenced by George Gershwin, is appropriately jazzy and urban, enhancing the show's streetwise atmosphere. Especially effective are Curtin's chase cues. Emphasizing strings, clarinet, and piano, these staccato cues complement the onscreen action.

The central character Top Cat is an unabashed rogue who conscientiously avoids honest work. But like Phil Silvers's Sergeant Bilko and Hanna-Barbera's earlier con artist Yogi Bear, he is amusing and likable. W.C. Fields, who played countless flimflammers on stage and screen, once said, "No one likes the fellow who is all rogue, but we'll forgive him almost if there is a warmth of human sympathy underneath his rogueries." Top Cat may not be human, but he certainly has warmth. When wangling, he never intends to hurt anyone or settle scores and he often schemes to help others. For instance, in the episode "A Visit from Mother," Benny the Ball is worried when he learns his mother will visit him; he wrote to her that he was the Mayor of New York! Top Cat and the other felines save Benny from embarrassment and his mother from disappointment by masquerading as big shots who know the Mayor. They take Benny's mother on a tour of the city that ends with a ticker tape parade they claim is for Benny. "A Visit from Mother" is both highly amusing and somewhat touching.

Top Cat even uses his conniving skills to help Officer Dibble solve crimes. In "Hawaii, Here We Come", Top Cat and the other felines are on a boat trip to Hawaii. Officer Dibble is also on the trip looking for a counterfeiter. Somehow, Top Cat and the gang find a suitcase full of phony bills and think they're genuine. The policeman catches them with the loot and accuses them of being counterfeiters. Top Cat clears his name *and* helps Officer Dibble catch the real crook by devising a trick to expose the culprit. The feline persuades the cop to tell the ship captain to announce that a suitcase full of money has been found. Everyone on board claims ownership except one passenger who tries to escape. It's a clever and funny resolution that demonstrates both Top Cat's craftiness and his essentially good heart.

Top Cat has never achieved the mass popularity of *The Flintstones* but its appealing characters and witty banter have ensured a loyal following to this very day. Like *The Flintstones* the show is easily obtainable on home video and on streaming. But at the time of *Top Cat*'s cancellation, these technologies were unavailable. Bill and Joe decided that funny animals were not profitable in primetime. Their next proposed primetime cartoon show would showcase humans, like *The Flintstones*. Unlike the Flintstones, these humans, the Jetsons, wouldn't engage in comical situations from the prehistoric past but in a speculative future.

Episode Guide for *Top Cat*

1"Hawaii, Here We Come" Airdate: September 27, 1961

When Benny wins a trip to Hawaii, Top Cat and the other felines accompany him by stowing away on the ship. Officer Dibble happens to be on the ship looking for a counterfeiter. Dibble discovers Top Cat and suspects him of being the counterfeiter and it is up to the feline to prove his innocence.

2"The Maharajah of Pookajee" Airdate: October 4, 1961

Top Cat poses as the Maharajah of Pookajee so he and his friends can enjoy all the amenities at a posh hotel but they get mixed up with crooks.

3"All That Jazz" Airdate: October 11, 1961

A new feline in town, A.T. (All That) Jazz, threatens Top Cat's dominance in the alley. Jazz takes charge of the pool hall, seduces Top Cat's girlfriend, and persuades Top Cat's gang to follow his orders. Top Cat connives to regain his leadership on his home turf.

4"The $1,000,000 Derby" Airdate: October 18, 1961

Benny befriends a camera-hogging horse. At first, Top Cat wants to get rid of the horse but when he learns the horse has alarm-induced racing abilities, he enters him in a derby.

5"The Violin Player" Airdate: October 25, 1961

Benny the Ball tries to take up the violin. The musical director of Carnegie Hall, Mr. Gutenbad, hears a professional violin recording and mistakes it for Benny's playing. He offers to pay the cat handsomely for performing at Carnegie Hall.

6"The Missing Heir" Airdate: November 1, 1961

Top Cat learns Benny is a dead ringer for "Cat-wallader", the missing heir to an enormous fortune. The gang succeeds in claiming the inheritance for Benny but they have to contend with the larcenous butler Chutney and his equally larcenous dog Griswald, who want the money for themselves.

7"Top Cat Falls in Love" Airdate: November 8, 1961

Top Cat goes to the hospital to visit tonsillectomy patient Benny. When he sets his eyes on the lovely cat nurse Miss LaRue there, Top Cat fakes an illness hoping she will tend to him.

8"A Visit from Mother" Airdate: November 15, 1961

When Benny learns his mother is coming to see him, he frets because he has written to her that he's the Mayor of New York. Top Cat and the gang use their conniving skills to make Mrs. Ball think her son is the actual Mayor.

9"Naked Town" Airdate: November 22, 1961

Officer Dibble permits Top Cat's alley to be used as shooting location for a warehouse robbery scene in the TV crime show *Naked Town*. But real criminals try to take advantage of this by committing an actual robbery on the set.

Note: "Naked Town" is play on the TV show *The Naked City*.

10"Sergeant Top Cat" Airdate: November 29, 1961

Top Cat overhears Officer Dibble's ideas to improve conditions to the police force and hoodwinks the Chief of the Police into believing these suggestions are Top Cat's. As a result, the feline is made an honorary police sergeant and Dibble's superior in the alley.

11"Choo-Choo's Romance" Airdate: December 6, 1961

When Choo-Choo gets infatuated with a gorgeous French cat, Goldie, Top Cat and the other felines help Choo-Choo to woo her. But the gang encounters a formidable obstacle- Goldie's possessive beau Pierre.

12"The Unscratchables" Airdate: December 13, 1961

Benny accidentally swallows a stolen diamond and is abducted by Big Gus and his mobsters who want to retrieve it. Top Cat and the gang try to come to Benny's rescue.

Note: The title is a play on the TV show *The Untouchables*.

13"Rafeefleas" Airdate: December 20, 1961

When Benny sleeps all night inside a museum, he gets a scarab attached to his back. When Top Cat discovers the jewel, he and the rest of the gang try to return to it. But a crook steals the scarab along with other jewels and Officer Dibble mistakes Top Cat for the thief.

14"The Tycoon" Airdate: December 27, 1961

Top Cat receives a check of a million dollars from a tycoon because the donor considers him the most unfortunate soul he has seen. He gives the check to Benny the Ball but word spreads around that Top Cat is a millionaire and everyone treats him like royalty.

15"The Long Hot Winter" Airdate: January 3, 1962

When winter arrives, Top Cat and the gang seek refuge from the cold in

Officer Dibble's house. The policeman has to endure living with the cats until the coming of spring.

16"The Case of the Absent Anteater" Airdate: January 10, 1962

Top Cat wants to get rid of Benny's new pet, a ravenous giant anteater. But when he learns the anteater has escaped from the zoo and there's a reward for his return, Top Cat tries to take advantage of this situation

17"T.C. Minds the Baby" Airdate: January 17, 1962

Top Cat and the gang adopt an abandoned human baby and struggle to take care of him.

18"Farewell, Mr. Dibble" Airdate: January 24, 1962

A new recruit named Ernest Prowler replaces Officer Dibble on the beat in Top Cat's alley. Prowler proves to be tougher on Top Cat and his friends than Dibble ever was so the felines scheme to get Dibble back.

19"The Grand Tour" Airdate: January 31, 1962

Top Cat's latest money-making scheme consists of a bogus "historical" tour of New York, complete with "phony" maps for sale. To Top Cat's surprise, these maps actually lead to a genuine treasure in a run down house.

20"The Golden Fleecing"Airdate: February 7, 1962

When Benny receives an insurance payment of $2,000, Top Cat takes advantage of it by taking him and the rest of the gang to a nightclub. The showgirl performing there, Honeydew Mellon, is part of a gang of poker-playing con artists and when they learn Benny is loaded, they try to get all his money.

21"Space Monkey" Airdate: February 14, 1962

After learning that a chimpanzee is treated like a king at Cape Canaveral's
space program, Top Cat and the gang decide to enlist there. But they
regret joining the program when they find out they'll be sent into
space.

22"The Late T.C." Airdate: February 21, 1962

Top Cat is beaned by a home run while watching a baseball game at Yankee
Stadium. At the hospital, he is diagnosed with nothing more serious
than a bump on the head. But when Officer Dibble arrives there to
check on Top Cat, he mishears the doctor and thinks the feline only has
a week to live. When Top Cat learns of Dibble's misunderstanding, he
takes advantage of it and has Dibble at his beck and call.

23"Dibble's Birthday" Airdate: February 28, 1962

When Officer Dibble's birthday's around the corner, the policeman worries
that he's getting too old. Top Cat and the gang try to lift his spirits
by holding a party for him with presents from all the neighborhood
denizens.

24"Choo-Choo Goes Ga-Ga" Airdate: March 7, 1962

Choo-Choo is in a suicidal frame of mind because he can't get a date with
Hollywood star Lola Glamour. Top Cat vows to fix up Choo Choo
with Lola. When he learns that Lola will only go out with someone
who's rich, he tries to pass off Choo Choo to her as Count Chooch, a
wealthy count.

25"King for a Day" Airdate: March 14, 1962

Top Cat and the gang go on the game show "King for a Day," hoping to win prizes. But Officer Dibble also goes on the show and winds up the winner.

26"The Con Men" Airdate: March 21, 1962

When an amiable hot dog vendor is robbed of $1,000 by con men pretending to own an oil well in Nova Scotia, Top Cat tries to get the money back. His scheme is to masquerade as wealthy Texan and convince the scoundrels *he* owns an oil well in Nova Scotia.

27"Dibble Breaks the Record" Airdate: March 28, 1962

In order to win a two-week vacation, Dibble is determined to break a record as the longest serving police officer on the beat. Top Cat and the gang see to it that Dibble doesn't miss a day of work so he'll get the vacation and the cats won't have to put up with him for two weeks.

28"Dibble Sings Again" Airdate: April 4, 1962

Top Cat hears Officer Dibble sing and persuades him that under his managment, he could become a big singing sensation. The feline isn't only interested in getting rich; he's in debt to loan shark Big Gus.

29"Griswald" Airdate: April 11, 1962

The dog Griswald shows up again as Dibble's new partner on the beat. The canine is a formidable adversary who constantly outwits Top Cat and his gang and the alley cats wonder how they can get rid of him.

30"Dibble's Double" Airdate: April 18, 1962

Top Cat decides to make a fortune in painting. Meanwhile a criminal called Al the Actor impersonates Officer Dibble to rob artworks- including Top Cat's.

The Jetsons

Broadcast Station: ABC. Telecast: September 23, 1962-September 8, 1963. Studio: Hanna-Barbera/Screen Gems. Produced and directed by William Hanna and Joseph Barbera. Animation director: Charles Nichols. Music by Hoyt Curtin. Written by Michael Maltese, Warren Foster, Harvey Bullock, Larry Markes and Tony Benedict. Voices: George O'Hanlon (George Jetson); Penny Singleton (Jane Jetson); Mel Blanc (Spacely); Daws Butler (Elroy Jetson/Cogswell); Janet Waldo (Judy Jetson); Don Messick (Astro); Jean VanderPyl (Rosie the Robot); and Howard Morris, John Stephenson, Hal Smith, Herschel Bernardi, Dick Beals, Joan Gardner, among others.

When the idea for *The Jetsons* was conceived in 1962, the U.S.A. was sending people into space. President John F. Kennedy promised that before the end of the 1960s, American astronauts would plant the country's flag on the surface of the moon. On February 20, 1962, John Glenn became the first American to orbit the earth. Americans were enthralled about the possibilities of not only traveling to but actually *living* in outer space, a utopian civilization among the stars. *The Jetsons* would find humor and entertainment in this speculative future. The show would also reflect Americans' rose-colored dream for society.

The Jetsons's time setting would be 2062, exactly one century after the year of its primetime debut. Imagining this period was challenging for Bill and Joe. Joe Barbera told reporter Hal Marshall:

> " 'The Jetsons' depicts family life in the future...There's only one hitch, the present keeps catching up with the future. The idea men come up with a new design for space travel or an imaginative home appliance for the 21st Century home. They get to use it in the show and then discover there is something in the works-somewhere in the world- similar...We had to scrap a lot of ideas. Speeds we planned on using were already being surpassed [in the 20th century]."

Joe Barbera told another reporter, Kay Gardella, about the same problems and she commented, "Listening to the producer, one could envision the headache Jules Verne would have if he were alive today. A book like 'Around the World in Eighty Days,' for instance, would probably undergo five title changes before it got off the presses."

Casting for the voices on *The Jetsons* was also a challenge. Morey Amsterdam and Pat Carroll were the first choices for the space age couple George and Jane Jetson. But at the time, both were regulars on live-action shows; Amsterdam on *The Dick Van Dyke Show* and Carroll on *The Danny Thomas Show*. They had to decline Hanna-Barbera's offer to avoid conflicts with the live action program sponsors.

The replacing actors, George O'Hanlon and Penny Singleton, had played popular characters in live-action films. Their film personas were tailor made for the roles of George and Jane Jetson. O'Hanlon had starred in a long-running short subject series called *Behind the Eight Ball*. He played Joe McDoakes, an ordinary guy in comically extraordinary situations. His light, innocent voice ideally suited George Jetson, as identifiable an Everyman as

Fred Flintstone. Singleton had played perky housewife Blondie Bumstead in a string of features based on Chic Young's popular comic strip *Blondie*. The same combination of wifely wisdom and girlish impulsiveness that made Singleton's Blondie amusing and memorable would voice Jane Jetson.

When Singleton was hired for *The Jetsons*, she was mired in tumultuous litigation. She was a brave and tireless crusader for the rights of chorus girls, antagonizing show business executives and mob-connected nightclub owners in the process. Singleton was burdened with lawsuits, which she defended by countersuing. She even testified at a Senate hearing investigating abuses by officials of the American Guild of Variety Artists. At the hearing, she denounced them for, according to press accounts, "conniving with night club owners to degrade and exploit run-of-the-mine exotic dancers and other entertainers." Penny's *Jetsons* salary helped financially sustain her during this turbulent time. The Senate hearing ruled in Singleton's favor and she won a settlement of $15,000. She continued to lobby on behalf of chorus girls, even organizing a strike by the Radio City Rockettes in 1966.

Unlike the Flintstones, who were childless until the middle of the 1962-63 season, the Jetsons would always be parents. Their daughter Judy was a typical teenage girl, easily excited and constantly having a crush on someone. Janet Waldo had played teenage girls on films and on radio for years, most notably the title role on the radio sitcom *Meet Corliss Archer*. Although she was in her forties when hired as Judy, her squeals and coos believably conveyed a far younger character. Waldo was also quite versatile and for several decades would provide a variety of voices on countless Hanna-Barbera cartoons.

The Jetsons would also have a precocious little boy named Elroy who enjoyed typical juvenile activities such as scouting. Lucille Bliss, who had voiced television's first cartoon star Crusader Rabbit back in 1949, was Hanna-Barbera's original choice for the part. The actress later claimed that director Alan Dinehart, Jr. told her to pass herself off in credits and publicity as a boy named "Lou Bliss." Lucille's agent Miles Auer objected, insisting that her real name should be used. As a result, Hanna-Barbera fired her. She was devastated by her firing but she got over the trauma and immersed herself in new voiceover projects. (Ironically, a few years later, she did voice work as a little boy on a Hanna-Barbera Saturday morning cartoon *Space Kiddettes* credited as "Lou Bliss.")

Bliss's replacement was not a boy but a man- Hanna-Barbera veteran Daws Butler. He was even older than Janet Waldo but he had already proven himself adept at sounding like a youngster when voicing Augie Doggie. As Elroy, he was as believably youthful as Waldo was as Judy. Butler later said, "Everybody [who watched *The Jetsons*] always assumed Elroy was a kid. For me, it's like self-hypnosis. You must convince yourself that you're...[a boy again], let the feeling go through your entire body."

Butler also got help playing Elroy- his own sons, who were children at the time. When he was working on the voice in his home recording studio, the boys provided suggestions on how to do it. One suggestion which Daws picked up was to rush through a line or underplay it, in Butler's words, "for his own satisfaction but so his father can't hear it." Daws also learned from his sons to misremember big words. Typical malapropisms were "idiotcyncracy" and "stupidstitious."

By listening not only to his sons' suggestions but observing their speech patterns, Butler was able to understand the children's thought processes. He explained to a reporter:

> "...Children's minds are flitty. If I tell one of the younger ones that I want to speak to him, he's apt to come up with something like, 'Wait a minute. I have to get the football.' Children aren't dishonest, but if there's a chance to weasel out, they will, because what is important to us is not to them..."

The Flintstones had a pet dinosaur that behaved like a dog so it made sense for Bill and Joe to give the Jetsons a pet dog. (Of course dinosaurs would be regarded as extinct in the future as they were in the year 1962.) Named Astro, this canine provided a substantial amount of the show's humor and heart. He was affectionate to a fault, slobbering and pawing all over George, to his master's annoyance. Hungry for love and attention, Astro would blubber if he was ignored. Don Messick provided a unique voice for Astro; in a gravely tone, he pronounced all his words with "r" at the first consonant. For example, when Astro said "How about that?" it sounded like "Row arout rat?" Messick would later do a similar voice for the Great Dane Scooby Doo, Hanna-Barbera's most profitable and durable character.

What would the future *look* like? Hanna-Barbera's artists imagined it as space oriented. They envisioned and drew buildings so tall they would literally reach the stars. They devised rockets and other flying vehicles in the galaxies as modes of transportation. To further illustrate this imaginary space age, the artists created a distinctive style for the characters and costumes. Bill Hanna recalled in his autobiography, "*The Jetsons* was distinctly airy in its design... The characters and costumes, along with the vehicles, props, and structures of the show, were drawn in a streamlined mode distinctly suggestive of what our artists envisioned as being the look of the distant future...the selection of colors used for the series...[were]...a whole...spectrum of celestial blues, metallic grays, and synthetic pastels in order to impart distinctly modern tones to the computerized and climatized world of *The Jetsons*."

The Hanna-Barbera staff also envisioned a future dependent on automated equipment, a time when manual effort wouldn't be as necessary. Joe Barbera saw to it that the characters would never walk; instead they would be whisked from place to place via conveyor belt and go through doors sliding open for them. Joe Barbera provided examples of the Jetsons' space age lifestyle to author Ted Sennett:

> "When George arrived and stepped on a people-mover, in a second he had Rosie the Robot waiting for him to take his coat or hat. The family dog Astro didn't have to be taken for a walk- he was just placed outside the house on a treadmill. That's how he got his exercise. The characters didn't even have to move to change their clothes- they would just stand in front of a cutout and in an instant, a new outfit would be superimposed on their bodies."

To create a futuristic setting ,the Hanna-Barbera staff studied modern architecture, particularly Googie architecture, an innovative style noted for dramatic sloping roofs and an emphasis on glass and steel. This style was especially popular in southern California in places like the Los Angeles International Airport's Theme Building and Disneyland's Tomorrowland (another speculative view of the future!). In conjuring up *The Jetsons*'s civilization, the artists were also inspired by serious books that contemplated tomorrow's society such as Arnold B. Barach and the Kiplinger Washington Editors' *1975: And the Changes to Come*.

How did Hanna-Barbera promote *The Jetsons*? The studio marketed the Jetsons as people everyone in the 20th century could identify with, even though they lived in the 21st century. One ad described the family as "Years ahead- but the Jetsons' domestic problems are not unlike your own!" Another declared, "Man in space! George Jetson heads a family of the future in a way of life very much like our own!" Joe Barbera explained to *Variety*, "We have taken families and their problems and moved them 100 years ahead. All the problems are basic ones. We try to answer everybody's thinking- 'I wonder what it's going to be like 100 years from now?' " To assure potential viewers *The Jetsons* would not be a dry speculation on what would happen to humanity, he said "if we get scientific, we're dead. We have to do it with fun." Hanna-Barbera also promoted the show by promising viewers futuristic gadgets to marvel at like a wall-to-wall television and a seeing-eye vacuum cleaner.

On September 23, 1962, the first episode of *The Jetsons* aired. On balance, the reviews were favorable. *Daily Variety*'s critic "Helm" wrote: "It's one of the rarities of television that a producing studio, using the same formula, can follow one hit with another. More to the credit of William Hanna and Joseph Barbera that it's a cartoon...By the simple device of looking ahead with *The Jetsons*, whereas 'Flinty' [*The Flintstones*] looks back into the Stone Age, they achieved a new delight for the young 'uns and plenty of [parents] looking over their shoulders in this early evening fun show..."

"Helm" may have considered *The Jetsons* fun for the average American family, but the average family had other options in the cartoon show's time slot. If they tuned in to NBC, they could watch *Walt Disney's Wonderful World of Color*. (At that time. color television was fairly new. *The Jetsons* was also broadcast in color.) If they checked CBS, they could see *Dennis the Menace*, the live-action adapation of the popular comic strip about a mischevious tyke. (Incidentally, this show was broadcast in black and white.) Joe Barbera was all too aware of *The Jetsons*'s formidable competition. He later told Ted Sennett, "When you have three family shows opposite each other, you're splitting your audience."

The ratings soon revealed that on the whole viewers preferred Walt Disney to the Jetsons. In 1962, Disney was already a living legend and a household word while the Jetsons were an unknown entity. It's also possible that viewers considered *The Jetsons* little more than a futuristic inverse of *The Flintstones* and that one cartoon family in a time displacement was enough. (An April 1963 article in *Television* magazine proposed this hypothesis.)

Another problem with *The Jetsons* was that it wasn't attracting enough adult viewers. Two of the show's three sponsors, Colgate, and Whitehall Labs, were represented by Ted Bates and Co. Bates's clients believed *The Jetsons* would be less lucrative if grown-ups didn't watch the show. After all, the adults held the family purse strings, not the youngsters. So Bates worked out a contract with Hanna-Barbera stipulating that the program entice a minimum of 15 million adults per average commercial minute for the first 26 weeks. If by the end of this period, the minimum wasn't achieved, Bates's clients would be compensated with commercial time during the program. The minimum wasn't achieved, discouraging important clients from investing in *The Jetsons*. The show was cancelled at the end of the 1962-63 season. (*Dennis the Menace* was also taken off the air.)

Like *Top Cat*, reruns of *The Jetsons* showed up on Saturday morning. And like *Top Cat*, *The Jetsons* attracted more viewers in this time slot than they did in primetime. George O'Hanlon would later say that his own children regularly watched the reruns for twelve years. In the mid 1980s, new episodes were devised for syndication. They were so popular that Hanna-Barbera came out with a theatrical feature in 1990. Sadly, by the time of the feature's release,

Daws Butler and George O'Hanlon had passed away. (Janet Waldo was still alive and well but she was unceremoniously dumped in favor of then-hot pop music sensation Tiffany.) Now available on home video and online streaming, *The Jetsons* is firmly imprinted in popular culture.

Watching *The Jetsons*'s primetime episodes today in the 21st century, one notes how in some ways they reflect culture and attitudes in the early 1960s. Popular entertainers of the day like Ed Sullivan, Dean Martin, and Soupy Sales are lampooned. Today, these figures are mere footnotes in show business history but more than half a century ago, they were household names. One unfortunate aspect of this era is the show's casual sexism. Jane Jetson is not only a housewife without any independent career goals, but she is passive and worries needlessly that her husband is fooling around. One especially insulting episode, the self-explanatory "Jane's Driving Lesson," perpetuates the stereotype of the lousy woman driver.

Even more troubling is the absence of nonwhite people on *The Jetsons*. In the wake of the civil rights struggles in the latter part of the 1960s, Hanna-Barbera inserted nonwhite characters in their cartoons and even had nonwhite cartoon stars such as their animated version of the all-black basketball team the Harlem Globetrotters. But in the early 1960s, racial minorities, especially blacks, were generally ignored by the television industry.

But if *The Jetsons* is dated in some aspects, the show is prescient in the future of technology. As Joe Barbera acknowledged, the show had no pretensions of taking a serious look at the civilization of tomorrow. But at least some of the show's devices, while regarded as science fiction in the early 1960s, have become reality. One notable gadget on the show is the "peek-a-boo" capsule, which when swallowed, transmits pictures of the ingester's internal organs, mirroring today's endoscopic cameras which are used to view a patient's digestive tract.

The humor on *The Jetsons* is uneven, ranging from clever satire, like the dumbing down of television, to jokes that were old hat even in 1962, such as cracks about nagging mothers-in-law. The human characters are amusing and likable but lack the depth of the people on *The Flintstones* and the flair of the felines on *Top Cat*. George Jetson in particular seems bland in comparison to Fred Flintstone. Unlike Fred Flintstone who is a working class individual striving for a better life for himself and his family, George Jetson is comfortably middle class. George does have to deal with a nasty boss and he's frustrated that he's never promoted, but it's hard to feel sorry for him when he only works three hours a day and just pushes buttons at work. Of course Hanna-Barbera's humorous point is that in the future, people won't have to work as hard,, but as a result, George's frustrations aren't as compelling as Fred's. And unlike Fred, George doesn't have a best friend he can confide in and share misadventures with.

Despite these shortcomings, *The Jetsons* remains delightful entertainment. One can understand why people have watched it for generations. If not all the futuristic gadgets on the show have become reality, they are still fun to watch not only because they are inventive but because one *believes* they could actually function in real life. The legendary Mel Blanc is a hoot voicing George's irascible boss Mr. Spacely. His gift for saying things funny is especially evident whenever he bellows at his unfortunate employee, "YOU'RE FIRED!" And Astro the dog is always a riot to watch. In fact, he is funnier and more colorful than any of the human characters.

Hoyt Curtin's musical score is another asset. It combines earthbound jazz, with an emphasis on brass, with spacebound science fiction music, particularly the use of the then new electric piano. (Synthesizers were not yet used in mass market music.) The energetic, breezy music channels the optimism for the future. When Curtin composed the theme song, he originally recorded it with a small band. But after receiving positive feedback, he decided to rerecord it with a larger band. Curtin later remembered, "I just had the musicians listen to, on headsets, the first tryout with a small band. I wrote an arrangement to include the large group, all the strings, and everything." But when *The Jetsons* stopped airing in primetime in 1963, Bill and Joe decided for the time being not to create any more animated sitcoms. *The Flintstones*'s popularity was genuine but it seemed to be a fluke. Hanna-Barbera did not devise any new primetime cartoons for the 1963-64 season.

In 1964, the studio decided to take a chance with a new program. But this program would not be a comedy. Instead, it would be a serious adventure series, a genre Hanna-Barbera had yet to explore.

Episode Guide for *The Jetsons*

1 "Rosey the Robot" Airdate: September 23, 1962

George invites his boss Mr. Spacely to his home for dinner, hoping to get a
raise. At the same time, Jane buys a robot maid named Rosey. Dinner
with the boss and the new maid doesn't go smoothly.

2 "A Date with Jet Screamer" Airdate: September 30, 1962

Judy idolizes pop sensation Jet Screamer but George cannot stand him.
To his chagrin, his daughter wins a contest resulting in a date with the
rock star.

3 "The Space Car" Airdate: October 7, 1962

George and Jane think of buying a new space car but they inadvertently get
involved with an escaped convict and his moll.

4 "The Coming of Astro" Airdate: October 14, 1962

Elroy finds a dog named Astro and brings him home. Everyone in the
family except George wants to adopt Astro. George will let Astro stay
if the dog proves himself to be more useful than a robotic dog George
has just bought.

5 "The Jetson's Nite Out" Airdate: October 21, 1962

Spacely has two tickets for a championship robot football game and gives
one of the tickets to George. George tells Jane he has to work late at
the office with Spacely to evade a prior commitment but both men get
into hot water when their wives find out they've been lying.

Note: Astro does not appear in this episode.

6"The Good Little Scouts" Airdate: October 28, 1962

George gets lost on the moon where he has taken Elroy's scout troop.

Note: Astro does not appear in this episode.

7"The Flying Suit" Airdate: November 4, 1962

Elroy tries to concoct flying pills. When George takes one, he can suddenly soar in the air. He doesn't realize that the actual source of his new ability is a newly manufactured flying suit.

Note: Astro does not appear in this episode.

8"Rosey's Boyfriend" Airdate: November 11, 1962

Rosey goes ga-ga over Mac, a mechanical assistant of Henry Orbit, the superintendent of the Jetsons' apartment.

Note: Astro is absent from this episode. This is Rosey's second and final appearance on the program. She is absent from all of the other episodes.

9"Elroy's TV Show" Airdate: November 18, 1962

A TV producer casts Elroy and Astro for his new show"Spaceboy Zoom and His Dog, Astro". George decides to be Elroy's manager and becomes an aggressive stage father.

10"Uniblab" Airdate: November 25, 1962

George expects to get a promotion but instead Spacely replaces him with an intelligent, bootlicking robot named Uniblab.

Note: Astro does not appear in this episode.

11 "A Visit from Grandpa" Airdate: December 2, 1962

George's overenergetic 110-year old grandfather Montague visits the Jetsons and wears them out with his antics.

12 "Astro's Top Secret" Airdate: December 9, 1962

Astro accidentally swallows Elroy's flying two car, giving *him* the power of flight. Harlan, a spy of Spacely's business rival Cogswell, sees the dog soaring in the air and is convinced that Jetson has created an anti-gravity device for his boss.

Note: Judy Jetson does not appear in this episode.

13 "Las Venus" Airdate: December 16, 1962

George goes on a second honeymoon with Jane to Las Venus. But Spacely Sprockets assigns him to see a beautiful female client named Gigi Galaxy there. Now George must divide his time between Jane and Gigi and tries not to arouse his wife's jealousy.

14 "Elroy's Pal" Airdate: December 23, 1962

Elroy 's idol, the TV superhero Nimbus the Great, turns out to have feet of clay.

Note: Astro does not appear in this episode.

15 "Test Pilot" Airdate: December 30, 1962

George erroneously believes he doesn't have long to live so feeling he has nothing to lose, he becomes a test pilot for an "indestructible" suit.

16"Millionaire Astro" Airdate: January 6, 1963

Astro turns out be be a used dog; his original name was Tralfaz and his original owner, millionaire J.P. Gottrockets, wants him back.

17"The Little Man" Airdate: January 13, 1963

When Spacely tests his new invention, the MiniVac, on George, he shrinks his employee to six inches high. The process can not be reversed because of a glitch in the machine's enlarging program. How can the machine be fixed? Mr. Spacely takes advantage of George's miniature size by sending him to steal one of the cogs from Cogswell Cogs.

18"Jane's Driving Lesson" Airdate: January 20, 1963

The title sums up what happens in the episode. But Jane's driving lesson does not go smoothly. In fact, she gets mixed up with a gangster.

19"G.I. Jetson" Airdate: January 27, 1963

When George is drafted for reserve training in the U.S. Space Guard, he discovers that both his demanding boss Spacely and the backstabbing robot Uniblab are his superiors.

20"Miss Solar System" Airdate: February 3, 1963

Jane is upset that George is so infatuated with Gina Lolajupiter (a spoof of Gina Lollobrigida) on television that he ignores her. She enters a beauty pageant her husband is judging to show up the other contestants.

Note: Judy and Astro are absent from this episode.

21"Private Property" Airdate: February 10, 1963

The opening of a new Cogswell Cogs office next door to Spacely Sprockets results in a new battle between Spacely and Cogswell. This time it's over property. Spacely claims that Cogswell's office is on his property. Therefore Cogswell should move his office. But after it's been discovered that George misread the blueprints, it is revealed that Spacely's office is on Cogswell's property. So Spacely is the one who is expected to relocate.

22"Dude Planet" Airdate: February 17, 1963

The dude planet is a place where Jane takes a vacation with her friend Helen. But she worries that her husband George is fooling around behind her back.

Note: The Jetsons' cat, seen in all the episodes' closing credits, makes its only appearance in the episode. The cat is bigger in "The Dude Planet" than it is in the closing credits. Curiously, Astro the dog is absent from this episode.

23"TV or Not TV" Airdate: February 24, 1963

When George and Astro notice the filming of a crime TV show called *The Naked Planet* (a spoof of *The Naked City*), they think they've seen an actual crime.

24"Elroy's Mob" Airdate: March 3, 1963

Elroy runs away from home when his parents mistakenly believe he received bad grades. (Another student, Kenny Countdown, has swiped Elroy's excellent report tape for his.) The boy unwittingly gets mixed up with gangsters.

Note: In class, Kenny Countdown is watching on his wristwatch television "the billionth rerun of *The Flintstones*."

Jonny Quest

Broadcast Station: ABC. Telecast: September 18, 1964-September 9, 1965. Studio: Hanna-Barbera/Screen Gems. Produced and directed by William Hanna and Joseph Barbera. Story director: Paul Sommer. Story supervisor: Arthur Pierson. Animation director: Charles A. Nichols. Animation supervisor: Irv Spence. Music by Hoyt Curtin and Ted Nichols. Voices: Tim Matthieson (Jonny Quest); Mike Road (Race Bannon); John Stephenson, Don Messick (Dr. Benton Quest); Don Messick (Bandit); Danny Bravo (Hadji); Vic Perrin (Dr. Zin/others); Cathy Lewis (Jezebel Jade); and Everett Sloane, Henry Corden, Sam Edwards, Keye Luke, Doug Young, among others.

Bill Hanna and Joe Barbera had grown up in the early 20th century on adventure stories. They read them avidly in the pulp magazines and comic strips, listened to them eagerly on the radio, and watched them intently in the movie theatres. Joe especially loved *Terry and the Pirates*, a comic strip by Milton Caniff about the exploits of an American lad named Terry Lee and his adult companions in the Far East. It thrilled him to read about their escapades in an exotic location like the Far East, battling colorful antagonists like the aptly named Dragon Lady. For a long time, Barbera dreamed of creating an action-adventure series like *Terry and the Pirates*. Now in the 1960s, he and Bill would realize this vision at their cartoon studio.

Hanna-Barbera's first idea for an action-adventure series was an animated adaption of the radio show *Jack Armstrong: All American Boy*. Like Terry Lee, Jack Armstrong faced dangers with his friends in faraway lands. But the cartoon studio couldn't get the rights to use the show's characters. One of the studio's animation writers, Lance Falk, said that Bill and Joe "realized that it might be better and give them more artistic freedom to just create their own characters from whole cloth." Original characters would also be more profitable for Hanna-Barbera since the studio would have exclusive rights.

A proposed title for Hanna-Barbera's new program was *The Saga of Chip Balloo*, but that sounded too frivolous for a dramatic action show. Then the studio considered another title, *Quest File 037*. (The adventurous sounding Quest was picked out of a Los Angeles phone book.) Finally, Hanna-Barbera settled on *Jonny Quest*, the name of the young protagonist. Jonny Quest was not only inspired by the comic strip character Terry Lee and the radio character Jack Armstrong, but by Jackie Cooper and Frankie Darro, youthful actors in 1930s films.

Like Terry Lee and Jack Armstrong, Jonny Quest would have company on his adventures. One of his companions would be his widowed father, scientist Dr. Benton Quest. Working for the U.S. government, he was assigned to explore scientific mysteries all over the globe. Dr. Quest always took his son along on these trips. Why was Benton Quest a widower? "We couldn't put Mother in the series," Joe Barbera told Charles Witbeck in the syndicated column *TV Key*, "then we'd get domestic again and Mother would be in the kitchen making sandwiches. We decided to get completely away from those homey scenes where even the dogs are obedient. Life isn't like that." How the role of mothers in the American families has changed in half a century!

Not that female characters were completely absent from the program. Appearing in two *Quest* episodes was a female mercenary named Jade (voiced by Cathy Lewis). An old flame of another *Quest* regular, Roger "Race"

Bannon, she was brave and assertive and not only capably aided the men against the villains but she even twice rescued *them*. Nor was she submissive to Race, chastising him for his rudeness. Jade was a strong character female viewers could identify with and admire. Attractively drawn with a slim figure, sleek black hair styled in a bun, and long eyelashes, she also appealed to male viewers. (Hanna-Barbera was noted for its curvaceous human female characters, exemplified by Wilma Flintstone and Betty Rubble on *The Flintstones* and Jane and Judy Jetson on *The Jetsons*.)

Who was Roger "Race" Bannon anyway? He served as both bodyguard and as Jonny's tutor. The character of Bannon was reminiscent of Doc Savage, a rugged hero in pulp magazines who had amazing strength and intelligence. Jonny Quest would also have a friend around his own age, an Indian boy, Hadji. The character of Hadji was inspired by Sabu, a youthful Indian actor in 1940s British and American films. Hadji was somewhat stereotyped as a mystic but he was intelligent and articulate and treated as an equal by Quest.

Hanna-Barbera's previous human characters, the Flintstones and the Jetsons, each had an animal companion. Jonny Quest and his friends would also have one. This critter would provide humorous relief from *Quest*'s suspense. Joe Barbera also felt an animal companion would be a marketable toy. Discussions were held envisioning an exotic creature like a monkey but a decison was made to make him a dog like the Jetsons' Astro. Black and white, he was named Bandit because the black area around his eyes resembled a burglar's mask.

Since *Jonny Quest* was intended to be a dramatic show, Bill and Joe realized that the obviously cartoonly style of drawing used for the previous humorous animated programs wouldn't suit their new program. A sober, realistic style used in adventure strips like *Terry and the Pirates* was needed for *Jonny Quest*. Hanna-Barbera hired Doug Wildey to design and develop the show's characters. Wildey was a gifted artist who had worked on action comic books and strips like *Hopalong Cassidy*, *The Saint*, and *Buffalo Bill*. In utilizing the same style he used in the comics for the program, Wildey rendered *Quest*'s areas and backgrounds in a solid black. He also employed shadows not only to give the show a gritty look but for dramatic effect.

The characters would rely on computer equipment to deal with the show's threats. Wildey studied magazines like *Popular Mechanics* and *Scientific American* to learn how to design believable gadgets. One example that seemed outlandish yet was somehow credible was a portable sonic projector that could produce ultrahighfrequency sound waves. The heroes used this device to cause an avalanche that defeated their foes. Wildey also brought in other experienced action cartoonists and trained them in animation. He was condescending toward Hanna-Barbera's veteran staff, calling them "Flintstones animators." In fact, some of them were skilled in creating realistic humans; they had worked on Walt Disney's visually exquisite 1959 animated feature *Sleeping Beauty*.

Action comics and technical magazines weren't the only influences on *Jonny Quest*. At the time of production, the public couldn't get enough of secret agent James Bond. The 1962 film *Dr. No* spawned an immensely profitable series where the suave hero saved the world from megalomaniacs. The titular villain Dr. No inspired the show's recurring villain, the mad scientist Dr. Zin.

Real youngsters were recruited for the voices of Jonny Quest and Hadji. Tim Matthieson (who as a successful adult actor changed his name to Tim Matheson) was sixteen when he was hired to play the titular character. His voice hadn't fully matured so he sounded credible as an eleven year-old. Danny Bravo was around Tim's age when he was hired to play Hadji. His voice was deeper than Matheson's but it was supposed to sound more mature, emphasizing Hadji's levelheadedness, contrasting with Jonny's impulsiveness.

Don Messick, the voice of the Jetsons' dog Astro, provided appropriate canine sounds as Bandit. Since Bandit was conceived as a realistic dog, he did not speak like Astro. But Messick's noises clearly telegraphed the dog's emotions, ranging from fear to determination to playfulness. Character actor Mike Road aptly employed a rugged, no-nonsense voice for the rugged, no-nonsense Race Bannon.

John Stephenson, who played Fancy Fancy on *Top Cat*, was Dr. Benton

Quest for the first five produced episodes. He personified both fatherly compassion and scientific sagacity. Bill and Joe decided, however, after the first five episodes were completed, that Stephenson's voice didn't sufficiently contrast with Road's; both actors had fairly deep voices. Don Messick replaced Stephenson as Dr. Quest for the rest of the produced episodes. Possessing a lighter vocal timbre, Messick expressed the same qualities of kindness and wisdom as Stephenson. He later told Ted Sennett that Dr. Quest was one of his favorite Hanna-Barbera characters: "It gave me the opportunity to do a straight character for a change."

Bill and Joe could promote a straight cartoon adventure as a change from the studio's usual comedy product. Joe, who took care of the studio's PR, emphasized this to the press, stretching the truth in the process. He told the Syracuse *Post-Standard* that *Jonny Quest* would "bring animated, up-to-date adventure to television for the first time" and would "feature an art style never seen before in animation." This realistic art style was never seen in Hanna-Barbera animation before, but it had been used in earlier animation, particularly Max Fleischer's theatrical cartoons based on the popular comic book *Superman*. But it was understandable that Barbera wanted to make *Jonny Quest* seem even more innovative than it was; production costs for the program were high and the studio was anxious to entice viewers. To lure viewers of all ages, Joe stressed that *Jonny Quest* was "designed to reach adults as well as children".

In hyping *Jonny Quest*, Barbera occasionally put his foot in his mouth. He told the press that the show would have no violence but that "due justice will come to each culprit in the 'cut suspenders-fallen pants' style'." Such slapstick style punishment was highly inappropriate for the show's villains, who were depicted as genuine threats. In fact, on the show the evildoers often died. They weren't deliberately killed and their demises were never shown, but viewers got the message that they paid horribly for their sins. Barbera must have worried about being criticized for suggesting violence. His worries were well founded; when the show aired, some people did criticize the show, fretting about its effect on younger viewers.

But when *Jonny Quest* premiered on September 18, 1964, it received a lot of praise from television reviewers. They didn't care that people got killed on this show because they considered the show itself to be skillfully constructed. Despite the concerns of some adults that *Jonny Quest* was too scary for the younger ones, the children, in the words of *Variety*, enjoyed "ogling the TV set." Yowp recalled watching the show as a child on his blog: "I was seven years old when the show debuted...Each week, I was gripped by the suspenseful and intense stories, augumented and enhanced by beautiful layouts and designs, and the unmatched musical work of Hoyt Curtin..."

In the comments section of another of Yowp's blogs about the show, one person reminisced:

> As a kid, I was impressed with the show and thought it was fantastic. The one episode that really scared me was the "Robot Spy" story. That thing was creepy, like a giant spider, and I was terrified of spiders. But I kept watching anyway, and of course Jonny and his father and friends triumphed. The entire show was kind of like that--startling visuals that made us return again and again for more.

Ratings for *Jonny Quest* were good during the fall of 1964. Unlike *Top Cat* and *The Jetsons*, this new show seemed to be a genuine hit. But while *Jonny Quest* was attracting viewers, Hanna-Barbera's earlier success *The Flintstones* was losing them. The studio's solution in December 1964 was to switch timeslots for their current shows. As mentioned before, *The Flintstones* benefited from the change, but *Jonny Quest* suffered. More people tuned in to CBS's *The Munsters* than they did to Hanna-Barbera's action series. Perhaps concerned parents wanted to shield their children from *Quest*'s implied violence; there was none of this on the whimsical *Munsters*. If parents hoped that *Quest* would be removed from primetime, their wish was fulfilled; the cartoon was cancelled by ABC at the end of the 1964-65 season.

There may have been another significant factor contributing to *Quest*'s early demise. One contributor in the comments section of one of Yowp's *Quest* blogs points out:

> ."..even when the switch was made, it didn't mesh with the shows that were around it -- half-hour comedies on both Thursday and Friday nights. It might have worked better if the network had bumped it back to run later in the evening, before a show like "Twelve O'Clock High" than in front of "The Addams Family" or "The Farmer's Daughter", but ABC was in the habit of airing their animated shows in the early 1960s during the opening hour of their nightly prime-time lineups, when kids were more likely to be around the TV, and so that's the treatment Jonny got, even though the tone was far different from H-B's other three half-hour comedies..."

Television executives felt *Quest* was for kids and they didn't share parents' concerns about the show: they aired reruns on Saturday morning for the next seven years. Like *Top Cat* and *The Jetsons*, the show did well in this time slot. In the 1980s, new episodes were aired in syndication. With the advent of home video and video streaming, people can now enjoy the original 1960s episodes. But do these episodes hold up in the 21st century?

In a word yes. *Jonny Quest* is enthralling escapist fun. The *look* of the show is impressive, with its meticulously rendered figures and gadgets and its painstakingly thorough backgrounds. The backgrounds are especially striking, an amazing variety showcasing the episodes's diverse locations like jungles, mountains, and deserts. Although like Hanna-Barbera's previous television product, the animation is limited, the timing of character movement is adroit, creating the *illusion* of full animation.

Complementing *Quest*'s stunning design is Hoyt Curtin's thrilling music score. Just as Hanna-Barbera's artists abandoned their usual cartoony designs for realistic ones to suit the show's dramatic format so did Curtin eschew his usual jaunty composing technique for a somber one. He skillfully utilized instruments, particularly trombones, to create *Quest*'s music, particularly the opening theme. This opener was perfectly attuned to exciting visual elements like a rampaging mummy and Benton's handling of a deadly weapon. Curtin's scoring was not entirely earnest; he used lighthearted music to accompany Bandit's comical antics. This whimsical musical interlude, like Bandit's capers, provided some welcome relief from *Quest*'s usual suspense. Curtin left Hanna-Barbera in the middle of the show's run. His replacement, Ted Nichols, smoothly sustained the score's intense atmosphere.

The characters of Jonny Quest and his friends are compelling not only because of the expert character design but also because of strong voice characterizations. Viewers care deeply about them and are alarmed when they are in danger. The relationship between Jonny and his father Benton is especially moving. In one episode, "Pursuit of the Po-Ho," Benton is abducted by Amazon savages called the Po-Hos to be used for ritual sacrifice. Jonny is not only frantic when he learns of this but determined to rescue his father no matter the peril. The boy's risking of his life to save his father shows the depth of his emotional bond.

Because of *Jonny Quest*'s impressive visual qualities and vivid characterizations, those who watched the show when it premiered remain fans today. It continues to attract new fans who weren't even born when it was in primetime. Had *Jonny Quest* been Hanna-Barbera's last primetime cartoon, the studio would have finished this time slot on a high artistic note. But a few years after *Quest*'s cancellation, Hanna-Barbera created a new primetime series that would be its least successful and most controversial.

Episode Guide for *Jonny Quest*

1"The Mystery of the Lizard Men" Airdate: September 18, 1964

Jonny, Dr. Quest, and Race Bannon investigate the mysterious
disappearance of five ships in the Sargasso Sea and in the process
discover a secret laser base. This base is being operated by a foreign
enemy power and is guarded by scuba divers disguised as lizard men to
frighten away potential intruders.

Note: Hadji is absent from this episode.

2"Arctic Splashdown" Airdate: September 25, 1964

Enemy agents sabotage a satellite missle which crashes into the Arctic.
Dr. Quest and his team arrive there to destroy the missle before the
enemies can utilize it for their own sinister purposes.

Note: Hadji debuts on this episode.

3"The Curse of Anubis" Airdate: October 2, 1964

Dr. Quest's treacherous friend Ahmed Kareem steals a valuable Egyptian
artifact and tries to frame Quest and Race for it. Unbeknownst to
Ahmed, his theft has aroused the wrath of a menacing mummy.

4"Pursuit of the Po-Ho" Airdate: October 9, 1964

The Po-Hos are a tribe of savage warriors in the Amazon jungle who have
kidnapped a scientist friend of Dr. Quest for ritual sacrifice. When Dr.
Quest tries to rescue his friend, the Po-Hos capture him and plan to
slaughter him as well.

5"Riddle of the Gold" Airdate: October 16, 1964

The nefarious Dr. Zin runs an alchemist counterfeit ring in India that manufactures gold. The Quests and their friends learn of this and go to India to investigate this racket.

Note: This is the first aired episode in which Don Messick does the voice of Benton Quest. This episode is also the first appearance of the Quests' recurring nemesis Dr. Zin.

6 "Treasure of the Temple" Airdate: October 23, 1964

The Quests and their friends go on an archeological trek to the ancient Mayan city of Malatan. While on the expedition, they confront a British scoundrel named Perkins, who is anxious to find treasure in the Mayan city.

7 "Calcutta Adventure" Airdate: October 30, 1964

Dr. Quest investigates a mysterious illness in India and in the process discovers a laboratory in a mountain. A megalomaniac named Kronick is using this laboratory to perfect a nerve gas which he will use to subdue anyone who stands in his way.

Note: This is a flashback episode, explaining how the orphan Hadji joined Dr. Quest, Jonny, and Race.

8 "The Robot Spy" Airdate: November 6, 1964

Dr. Quest works on creating a para-power ray gun, a weapon that can disempower any object and disarm any army or air force. Determined to steal the formula for this weapon, Dr. Zin utilizes a robot spy to do the dirty work.

9 "Double Danger" Airdate: November 13, 1964

Dr. Quest leads an trek in Thailand to find a medicinal vine. Dr. Zin covets the vine for his own evil purposes so he sends a henchman disguised as Race Bannon to infiltrate Dr. Quest's procession.

10"Shadow of the Condor" Airdate: November 20, 1964

When Dr. Quest's group makes an emergency landing in the Andes mountains, they meet Baron Heinrich von Frohleich, a veteran World War I German fighter ace who stores his planes in a castle. The Baron challenges Race to an aerial dogfight.

11"Skull and Double Crossbones" Airdate: November 27, 1964

Quest hires a cook named Jose and takes him along on a research ship in the Caribbean Sea. Jose turns out to be a spy for Mexican pirates who covet a sunken treasure Jonny has found.

12"The Dreadful Doll" Airdate: December 4, 1964

Dr. Quest and his team investigate alleged voodoo on a Caribbean island. They learn that the supposed voodoo is orchestrated by criminals who are running a secret submarine base. The crooks don't want any inhabitants to interfere with their operation so they are trying to scare them off the island.

13"A Small Matter of Pygmies" Airdate: December 11, 1964

On a trip to Dr. Quest's laboratory, Jonny and his companions are forced to land in the jungle when their plane has engine trouble. There, they confront a tribe of belligerent Pygmies and it's up to Dr. Quest to save his son and friends.

14"Dragons of Ashida" Airdate: December 18, 1964

The Quests and their friends visit a zoologist friend named Dr. Ashida.

To their shock, Dr. Ashida has not only gone mad, but he is breeding gigantic and dangerous reptiles.

15"Turu the Terrible" Airdate: December 25, 1964

On an expedition to find a rare metal to use in the space program, the Quests and their companions find a Pteranodon. They learn that this prehistoric creature has been trained by a slave driver to intimidate the natives to toil in his mining operation for the same metal.

16"The Fraudulent Volcano" Airdate: December 31, 1964

Dr. Quest invents a new fire bomb and uses it on an erupting volcano in a tropical Pacific island. He and his friends learn that Dr. Zin has been causing the eruptions because he is testing a deadly weapon.

17"Werewolf of the Timberland" Airdate: January 7, 1965

The Quests and their friends explore a Canadian forest for petrified wood but encounter unscrupulous lumberjacks in charge of a gold-smuggling operation. One of the lumberjacks has been trying to frighten away interlopers by disguising himself as a werewolf.

18"Pirates from Below" Airdate: January 14, 1965

Dr. Quest is working on an undersea prober for the United States Navy but a gang of international criminals try to seize it.

19"Attack of the Tree People" Airdate: January 21, 1965

When Jonny and Hadji's boat catches fire, the boys find refuge on the jungle coast on an African island. There, a pair of Australian ex-gunrunners try to aduct Johnny and Hadji for ransom but the crooks are foiled by a tribe of benevolent apes.

20 "The Invisible Monster" Airdate: January 28, 1965

When experimenting with molecular energy on Cavern Island, Dr. Quest's friend Isiah Norman accidentally creates an invisible monster that consumes him. The Quests and their friends use their wits and scientific expertise to destroy the menace.

21 "The Devil's Tower" Airdate: February 4, 1965

Exploring a plateau on the African continent, the Quest party discovers prehistoric men who are enslaved to mine diamonds by Klaus Heinrich von Dueffel, an escaped Nazi war criminal.

22 "The Quetong Missile Mystery" Airdate: February 11, 1965

Dr. Quest investigates the Quetong swamp in China to determine why the marine life there is making the fishermen ill. He discovers the source of the poison is fuel from a secret missle base run by a renegade general.

23 "The House of Seven Gargoyles" Airdate: February 18, 1965

The Quests, Hadji, Race, and Bandit visit Professor Erikson in Norway. The professor demonstrates to his guests his new invention, an anti-gravity device. But a gang of thieves led by Ivar tries to steal it and they employ a small-statured cat-burglar who disguises as one of the gargoyles on the tower of Erikson's castle.

24 "Terror Island" Airdate: February 25, 1965

On an island in Hong Kong, a malevolent scientist named Chu Sing Ling wants to perfect a formula to create giant animals. Anxious for Dr. Quest's help on the experiment, he abducts him.

25 "Monster in the Monastery" Airdate: March 4, 1965

In Nepal, the Quest party meets their friend Raj Guru, the high priest of

Khumjung. But Raj is threatened by terrorists who disguise themselves as Yeti, or abonimable snowmen.

26 "The Sea Haunt" Airdate: March 11, 1965

The Quests and their friends find a deserted freighter ship; not only do they wind up stranded on it, but they contend with a dangerous sea monster.

The New Adventures of Huckleberry Finn

Broadcast Station: NBC. Telecast: September 15, 1968-September 7, 1969. Studio: Hanna-Barbera. Produced and directed by William Hanna and Joseph Barbera. Directed by Charles Nichols. Music by Ted Nichols. Background art by Walt Peregoy. Cast (live-action): Michael Shea (Huckleberry Finn); Kevin Schultz (Tom Sawyer); Lu Ann Haslam (Becky Thatcher); Ted Cassidy (Injun Joe); Dorothy Tennant (Mrs. Thatcher- first episode); Anne Bellamy (Aunt Polly- first episode). Voices: Ted Cassidy, Dennis Day, Hal Smith, Ted DeCorsia, Peggy Webber, Jack Kruschen, Paul Stewart, Mike Road, Vic Perrin, Charles Lane, Julie Bennett, Paul Frees, Marvin Miller, Joe Sirola, Keye Luke, Janet Waldo, John Myhers, Henry Corden, Don Messick, Daws Butler, Bernard Fox, Danny Bravo, Dayton Lummis, Jay Novello, Abraham Sofaer, Than Wyenn, Bill Beckley.

When ABC cancelled *The Flintstones* at the end of the 1965-66 season, the Hanna-Barbera studio temporarily abandoned primetime shows to create new cartoons for the Saturday morning slot. However, the studio did not completely relinquish primetime. On February 26, 1967, NBC aired *Jack and the Beanstalk*. Starring the legendary song-and-dance man Gene Kelly, this TV special was the first to combine animation with live-action. The live-action segment was the "real" world of Jack (Bobby Riha) and his adult friend Jeremy (Kelly). The cartoon segment was the world of the beanstalk and its inhabitants up in the clouds. When Jack and Jeremy explored this upper world, they remained live-action. Through adroit special effects work, their flesh and blood figures were superimposed over animated backgrounds and they appeared to interact with animated characters, particularly the menacing Giant. Hanna-Barbera hired some new personnel to accomplish this wizardry. It wasn't easy but the results were glorious.

Jack and the Beanstalk not only was a hit with viewers but it won an Emmy for Outstanding Children's Program. Encouraged by the special's success. the Hanna-Barbera studio contemplated doing a regular primetime series combining live-action with animation for NBC. Joe Barbera explained to reporter Hal Humphrey how such a project would appeal to both children and adults: "When you say the word 'cartoon,' people think of children only, and we limit ourselves- although plenty of adults watch cartoons. We think combining the live action with the animation will give our company a special identification."

Like *Jack and the Beanstalk*, Hanna-Barbera's live action-animation combo would be based on a popular story. Instead of a fairy tale, however, the studio decided to use Mark Twain's *The Adventures of Huckleberry Finn* as a literary source for their project. The show was conceived as a continuation called *The New Adventures of Huckleberry Finn*. The premise was that Injun Joe, the villain in Twain's *The Adventures of Tom Sawyer* (published before *The Adventures of Huckleberry Finn*), escaped from prison, determined to punish Huck and Tom Sawyer for testifying against him in a murder trial. (This proposed conflict ignored the fact that Injun Joe perished in *The Adventures of Tom Sawyer*.) When the scoundrel pursued the boys, along with Tom Sawyer's sweetheart Becky Thatcher, they all wound up in a time warp.

Each episode would find the three children in an otherworldly place. The protagonists remained live-action but all the places (along with their inhabitants) they found themselves in were animated. Injun Joe became a cartoon and, still hell-bent on revenge, would assume a disguise in every animated terrain. It boggles the mind that Hanna-Barbera would take Twain's characters out of their Missouri riverfront milieu and plop them in a fantasy world.

In fairness to Hanna-Barbera, *The New Adventures of Huckleberry Finn* wasn't the first vehicle that utilized Twain's Mississippi River youths in a fantastic setting. Back in the 1940s, cartoonist Clare Victor Dwiggins conjured up outlandish adventures for Huck and Tom in the comics. Injun Joe was a frequent adversary in his comic strip *Huckleberry Finn* and Huck and Tom dealt with pirates, cannibals, and flying contraptions in the comic book *Supersnipe Comics*. One such story was the self descriptive "Huckleberry Finn Meets an Octopus on the Floating Island." But television, especially in primetime, was a more powerful and popular medium than the comics in the late 1960s. Bill and Joe were already handling a hot potato with their concept of *The New Adventures of Huckleberry Finn* before it aired.

Undertaking *The New Adventures of Huckleberry Finn* was not only controversial, but costly. This wasn't a one-shot special like *Jack and the Beanstalk* but a weekly series. Hanna-Barbera had to hire additional personnel so that this live action-animation combo could be accomplished. It was also a great challenge to find actors for the roles of Huckleberry Finn, Tom Sawyer, and Becky Thatcher. Three people were selected for a screen test shown to NBC executives in New York City. The executives believed the selected actors were too old so Hanna-Barbera launched a new talent search.

Over 1,300 boys auditioned for the part of Huckleberry Finn. 14-year old Michael Shea won the role. He had considerable experience on television, having guest starred on a variety of shows like *The Fugitive*, *Mission: Impossible* and *Bewitched*. (As previously noted, Hanna-Barbera had provided the animated opening titles for the latter show.) 13-year old Kevin Schultz was hired to play Tom Sawyer. Like Shea, he was already a veteran on television. Schultz had even been a regular on the Western series *The Monroes*. 14-year old LuAnn Haslam, who got the part of Becky Thatcher, was a comparative newcomer whose only professional acting experience had been in television commercials.

The towering, booming voiced character actor Ted Cassidy was cast as the villianous Injun Joe. He had done the voice of the animated Giant in *Jack and the Beanstalk* but was best known as the zombielike butler Lurch on the horror sitcom *The Addams Family*. (Hanna-Barbera later produced two Saturday morning cartoon versions of the show, the first in the 1970s and the second in the 1990s.) Although the part made Cassidy a celebrity, he considered it artistically stifling. He said to a reporter that as Lurch "there really wasn't much to do except walk around and...well, be Lurch." He was excited, however, to play Injun Joe in the upcoming *The New Adventures of Huckleberry Finn*: "I'm looking forward to it; I think I'll get more of a chance to do some acting than I did in *Addams*."

Now that Hanna-Barbera had hired the young people to play the live-action roles, the studio began to shoot their footage before combining it with animation. How did Hanna-Barbera manage this in the days long before computer-generated imagery? Well, the teenagers acted in front of a blue backdrop and the animation was added later. The dazzling onscreen result was the spectacle of flesh-and-blood people wandering across pen-and-ink scenery. If the live-action actors looked like they were performing on a designed stage set, that was the studio's intention. Hanna-Barbera wanted to give viewers the impression Huck, Tom, and Becky were exploring a surrealistic dream world. And the staff accomplished this remarkable feat. Background artist Walt Peregoy pointed out in an interview in *Animato!* magazine: "The mistake would try to be [*sic*] to integrate the animated background, and make the illustration an attempt at photographic realism. Then you'd have trouble. Because then you're trying to fool, and this doesn't work."

Even though the youths were the only actors on the set, they had to convincingly behave as if they were interacting with cartoon characters. Michael Shea later provided one example how this thespian technique was accomplished: "Injun Joe, for instance, was a cartoon character, so when I had to talk to him, I'd run my eyes slowly up the blue screen until the director told me to stop. Then I'd just try to remember where that point on the screen was."

In order to look believable exchanging dialogue with the nonexistent cartoon characters, the teenagers were assisted by a veteran character actor name Bruce Watson. Watson would not only deliver all of the cartoon characters's lines on the set, but act out all the roles, with a different voice for each one. Michael Shea recalled that he was so absorbed in playing a lion that he didn't notice for a while that the director had stopped the scene. After continuing to growl and roll on the floor for a while, Watson looked up and saw everybody staring at him. Shea commented, "He must have thought it was an awfully long lion scene."

Professional actors did the cartoon voices in a recording booth after live-action filming ended. Their voices were incorporated into the soundtrack accompanying the animation. It took six months to complete the animation for each episode. It took four hours to finish live-action shooting for each episode. What slowed down the shooting was that, according to California state law, the teenagers had to attend school for three hours a day with periods of instruction for at least 20 minutes at a time. They'd get into their costumes and then have lessons while the shot was being established. Luckily, everyone was taking the same courses, so they were all tutored together.

Eventually, all twenty episodes of *The New Adventures of Huckleberry Finn* were completed in time to be aired in the 1968-69 season. The show premiered on September 15, 1968 on NBC. Reviews were mixed. Some critics took the show to task for not being faithful to Mark Twain's text. One such scathing review was by Kathy Brooks in the *Telegram News Service*:

> "...no parent worth his salt should let his offspring think the TV version is the real Twain, or the real Becky or Tom or Huck. Shame on Hanna-Barbera. They've taken the characters, and in reverse Twain tradition, white-washed them into into fine upstanding citizens with no deviltry, and no charming original thoughts.

> Michael Shea plays Huck, and a more freshly-scrubbed looking

Huck would be hard to find; Kevin Schultz plays Tom, and ditto for him....it seems a shame Mark Twain couldn't rise up and throw the whole idea smack into the Mississippi."

Other critics, however, gave *The New Adventures of Huckleberry Finn* a somewhat positive reception. They seemed to be praise it, however, not because they were impressed with its artistic qualities but because they believed children would enjoy the program. For example, Wade Crosby in the Milwaukee *Journal* wrote, "Aside from the character names...there's no relation to anything Mark Twain put on paper. But it has built-in values that might make it a grabber for the taffy apple crowd." Such reviews revealed that some critics felt that adults would not be interested in the program.

Evidently, very few people of any age were interested in the program. According to the Chicago *Tribune*, the Nielsens revealed that out of 86 programs for the week of September 15, *The New Adventures of Huck Finn* ranked at the bottom, at number 86. The show had formidable competition on the other networks- *Lassie*, currently in its fifteenth season on the air, and Irwin Allen's science fiction show *Land of the Giants*. It's possible that many American parents discouraged their children from watching a program that in their view trashed Mark Twain's classic literature. There were complaints that young viewers would get a mistaken impression about Twain's characters from the show and ignore the books.

The Adventures of Huckleberry Finn and *The Adventures of Tom Sawyer* were not the only misused literary works on the program. In conjuring up the various fantasy lands for the protagonists, Hanna-Barbera purloined aspects of other classic stories. For example, one episode, "The Little People," placed Huck, Tom, and Becky in Lilliput, the tiny kingdom in Jonathan Swift's *Gulliver's Travels*. The political satire in Swift's original story was ignored in favor of conventional adventure.

Another episode, "Huck of La Mancha," teamed up the teenagers with Miguel de Cervantes's famous literary characters Don Quixote and his servant Sancho Panza. Cleveland Amory in *TV Guide* was especially incensed with that episode. He was appalled by the way Hanna-Barbera presented Cervantes's hero: "...it was really shocking to find that there was, in the concept of the character of Don Quixote, not one single whit of pathos, understanding, or even point." Amory was also disturbed at how Twain's and Cervantes's characters were exploited for hack melodramatics, such as in a sequence where Injun Joe (using the alias "Don Jose' D'Indio") tortured Sancho Panza to reveal the source of his master's wealth. To Amory, this sequence exemplified how "the whole thing does exactly the opposite of what it should do- i.e., bring to the child of today, if not the values and virtues of yesterday, at least the simple sanities."

Amory needn't have worried about *The New Adventures of Huckleberry Finn*'s detrimental effects on the mentality of American youth. Not only did the show continue to suffer from low ratings, but NBC often preempted it for sports events and specials. Predictably, the show was axed at the end of the 1968-69 season. Unlike Hanna-Barbera's other primetime cartoons, *The New Adventures of Huckleberry Finn* was not rerun on Saturday mornings.

It did get rerun in syndication in the late 1970s, but not as a stand alone program. Instead, it was aired as a section of another rerun program, the Saturday morning hit *The Banana Splits*. Originally run on NBC from 1968 to 1970, *The Banana Splits* had live action segments of people in outlandish animal costumes doing sketches, making music, and introducing cartoons. Now a decade later, these flesh-and-blood creatures introduced young viewers to segments of *The New Adventures of Huckleberry Finn*.

Complete episodes of *The New Adventures of Huckleberry Finn* did not remerge on television until the 2000s when they were aired on the nostalgic cable channel Boomerang. Finally in 2016, all of the episodes were issued on home video. Viewed today, is the show as awful as its detractors contended a half a century ago?

As an adaptation of Mark Twain's works, the show *is* a genuine travesty. Both *The Adventures of Tom Sawyer* and *The Adventures of Huckleberry Finn* are specifically stories of life in 1840s riverfront Missouri. Twain grew up in this region and his memories of his youth there inspired these books. *The*

Adventures of Huckleberry Finn in particular is not only a historical portrait of this milieu but a devastating satire of the inhabitants's mores and foibles. As historian Hal Erickson pointed out, by taking Twain's characters out of this Midwestern environment and hurling them into outlandish situations, they have been reduced to the level of any garden variety superhero or funny animal on Saturday morning TV.

The character of Huckleberry Finn suffers the most from Hanna-Barbera's cavalier treatment. David Hofstede points out on his blog Comfort TV, "Michael Shea's Huck is not the crude outcast Twain envisioned, but a wide-eyed, easygoing country boy given to explanations of 'Criminy!' while fleeing from Mongol hordes or Egyptian mummies." Lu Ann Haslam's Becky Thatcher doesn't fare much better. She exhibits some of the sharp intelligence that attracted Tom Sawyer in Twain's original work, but more often is reduced to a passive figure watching Tom and Huck battling villains and cheering them on. Kevin Schultz's Tom Sawyer comes off as the least scathed of Twain's youths, retaining at least some of the impish spunk from the books.

But if today's viewers approach *The New Adventures of Huckleberry Finn* without thinking of Twain's source material, they can often enjoy it as escapist entertainment. Even by today's standards, the combination of animation and live action is impressive. The cartoon backgrounds in particular are highly attractive and meticulously detailed.

There are some delightful segments that linger in the memory long after other segments are forgotten. For instance, in the premiere episode, "The Magic Shillelah," Twain's youngsters find themselves in a land of leprechauns. Becky and the leprechauns actually perform a number where the live-action girl dances while the leprechauns sing. Dennis Day provides lead vocal in a charming Irish brogue. This sequence has nothing to do with Twain but like the song and dance segments in the earlier special *Jack and the Beanstalk*, it demonstrates the Hanna-Barbera staff's skill in presenting live action/cartoon combo musical scenes.

Occasionally, the scenarists infuse the protagonists' plight with emotional resonance. In one episode, "The Curse of Thut," when the characters seem doomed, Huck laments that unlike Tom Sawyer and Becky Thatcher, he doesn't have a caring parent or guardian who will mourn him. In another episode, "The Gorgon's Head," Huck and Becky reflect on how long they've been away from Missouri. If *The New Adventures of Huckleberry Finn* had provided more thoughtful scenes like this, the youngsters' situation would have been more compelling.

The various animated guises of Injun Joe are impressively intimidating. All of these masquerades are presented as gigantic figures with severe, elongated visages, fierce scowls, and intense eyes. Ted Cassidy's deep, sepulchral voice perfectly matches his menacing appearance. The one major liability of this villain, though no fault of Cassidy's, is that he lacks any shading. Seeing him in one episode after another in a row, his threats and rages get a little monotonous.

Ted Nichols' music is another asset. Skillfully handling a full orchestra, with an emphasis on brass, strings, and woodwinds, he provides the show with more gravitas than it deserves. The underscore is especially effective in the program's suspenseful moments, thrilling and chilling to the ear. The music would be recycled on subsequent Hanna-Barbera Saturday morning cartoons, particularly *Scooby Doo Where Are You?*

Overall, *The New Adventures of Huckleberry Finn* is forgettable. One is sufficiently diverted when watching the program but on the whole isn't emotionally invested in the protagonists. If the viewer isn't familiar with Mark Twain's original works, he or she doesn't really care for the characters because there's little information about them before they plunge into the time warp. If the viewer *is* familiar with Mark Twain's original works, he or she finds that the characters don't measure up to the author's creations. Of all the 1960s primetime cartoons produced by Hanna-Barbera, *The New Adventures of Huckleberry Finn* is the least distinctive.

Episode Guide for *The New Adventures of Huckleberry Finn*

1"The Magic Shillelah" Air date: September 15, 1968

Huck, Tom, and Becky meet a group of leprechauns who are searching for their lost Magic Shillelah. Becky finds it but the gypsy chieftain Zarko (Injun Joe in disguise) not only takes it but abducts Tom and Huck. Becky and the leprechauns rescue the boys and reclaim the Shillelah.

2"Huck of La Mancha" Air date: September 22, 1968

The youngsters find themselves in the land of Don Quixote de la Mancha. Quixote's squire Sancho Panza has been kidnapped by a group of avaricious brigands. Huck, Tom, and Becky aid Quixote in rescuing Panza and defeating the brigands and their leader Don Jose (a.k.a. Injun Joe).

3"The Terrible Tempered Kahleef" Air date: September 29, 1968

All women in the city of Baghistan fear its despot Kahleef (an alias for Injun Joe) because he's determined to capture them and do away with them. Becky becomes Kahleef's latest hostage but Tom and Huck figure out a way to save her with the helped of a retired sorcerer named Muzaffar.

4"The Little People" Air date:October 6, 1968

The children get marooned on Lilliput. Separated from his friends, Huck is captured by the Lilliputians and their king wants him to marry his daughter. Meanwhile, Tom and Becky save two more Lilliputians and team up with them to save the land from a band of savages and their leader, the disguised Injun Joe.

5 "Pirate Island" Air date: October 13, 1968

Tom, Huck and Becky land on an island and discover that apes dwell there. A pirate named Captain X (a.k.a Injun Joe) and his band of buccaneers arrive on the island and kidnap Tom and Becky. But with the assistance of an ape named Bulu, Huck is able to help the other children defeat the pirates. Captain X's ship blows up but the youngsters escape from the vessel in the nick of time.

6 "The Last Labor of Hercules" Air date: October 20, 1968

Wandering in the woods, the youngsters run into Hercules, who is working on his last labor. The wicked king (Injun Joe again) and his centaur servant are determined to thwart Hercules's chances of succeeding in his task. With the help of the winged horse Pegasus, Huck, Tom, and Becky foil the king's scheme and Hercules is able to finish the final labor.

7 "The Gorgon's Head" Air date: October 27, 1968

Trekking through a cave, Tom, Huck and Becky discover a maiden shackled to an altar. They free her so she won't be sacrificed to a fire-breathing dragon. The Guru (a.k.a Injun Joe) imprisons the youngsters for liberating the maiden. The Guru's minion frees Tom, Huck and Becky and tells them the dragon can be turned to stone. But the only way to accomplish this is to use the head of a Gorgon. The youngsters succeed not only in stopping the dragon but in rescuing the maiden.

8 "The Castle of Evil" Air date: November 3, 1968

Injun Joe assumes the guise of a wizard named Zilbad who lives in a castle and commands skeleton warriors. These warriors abduct Becky but the boys rescue her. Huck uses guile to make a crystal statue out of Zilbad, thus undoing the wizard's spells.

9"Hunting the Hunter" Air date: November 24, 1968

Talking animals who hate humans put the youngsters on a judgement trial.
The beasts overcome their hostility when they ally with Huck, Tom,
and Becky against a human hunter (a.k.a. Injun Joe).

10"The Curse of Thut" Air date: December 1, 1968

Thut is a mummy who for five thousand years has been looking for his
lost love Marna. When Tom, Huck, and Becky are imprisoned by the
malevolent Typhonian Pharoah (Injun Joe again), the mummy not
only rescues them but he finds Marna.

11"The Ancient Valley" Air date: December 15, 1968

The youngsters stumble into the middle of a war in a prehistoric valley.
A rock-throwing tribe battles a spear-throwing tribe. Injun Joe
masquerades as a chieftain of a mountain tribe who wants to enslave the
two other tribes. The rock-throwers and spear-throwers temporarily
put aside their hostilties to aid Huck, Tom, and Becky in defeating the
mountain tribe.

12"Menace in the Ice" Air date: December 22, 1968

Injun Joe's guise is Captain Calidor and he shanghais Tom, Huck and
Becky. His plot to melt the snowland glaciers is foiled by the trio with
the help of Abominable Snowmen and Calidor's rebellious servant
Huga.

13"The Eye of Doorgah" Air date: December 29, 1968

Tom and Huck search for a gem called the Eye of Doorgah, which has
been stolen from a temple. A Thuggee clan led by Injun Joe in disguise
captures the boys but they escape, find the gem, and return it to the
temple. Doorgah punishes the Thugee clan.

14"Mission of Captain Mordecai" Airdate: January 5, 1969

Injun Joe masquerates as another sea captain, Captian Mordecai. He is
hunting an enormous whale. The youngsters board his ship and then
wind up swallowed by the whale. Huck, Tom, and Becky get out the
whale through its blowhole.

15"The Jungle Adventure" Air date: January 19, 1969

The youngsters find themselves in a jungle where an Anatrata bush poisons
Tom. He is then abducted by tribal warriors while Huck and Becky get
trapped on a slave-trading ship commanded by a disguised Injun Joe.
But Huck and Becky escape from the ship and get a cure for Tom in
the nick of time.

16"Son of the Sun" Air date: January 26, 1969

The Aztecs and their High Priest (a disguised Injun Joe) in their city declare
Tom is the Sun King. He relishes being monarch but he's expected to
jump from a tower and fly into the sky. Fortunately, Huck and Becky
rescue him before he plunges to his death and all three flee the city.

17"Prophecy of Peril" Air date: February 2, 1969

Injun Joe assumes the role of Xaon, the All-Powerful Khan of the Mongols.
Under his malevolent leadership, the Mongols plan to attack a Chinese
prince when he leaves the walled city where he lives. The youngsters
foil the ambush and save the prince. But the Mongols capture Tom,
Huck and Becky. The Mongols build a Trojan horse to transport to the
city and put Tom in it. A dog helps Huck and Becky escape. As for
Tom, he flees in a dragon kite and succeeds in destroying the Mongol
camp.

18"Strange Experiment" Air date: February 9, 1969

Tom, Huck and Becky take refuge in the house of a charming man named Dr. Filostro. But he turns out to be a mad doctor who keeps a dangerous beast (a.k.a. Injun Joe) and has a formula that can shrink living things. Huck temporarily falls victim to Filostro's concoction. Eventually, Tom and Becky manage to get their friend back to his normal size. As for Filostro, his assistant Creech, and the beast, they end up shrunk by the mad doctor's formula.

19"The Conquistador Curse" Air date: February 16, 1969

Huck, Tom, and Becky find gold in ancient Incan ruins. When they grab the riches and try to run off with them, they incur the wrath of a cursed Conquistador (a.k.a. Injun Joe) and he puts a spell on them. When they lose all of gold they are freed from the Conquistador's spell.

20"All Whirlpools Lead to Atlantis" Air date: February 23, 1969

After getting sucked down a whirlpool, Tom, Huck and Becky find themselves in the underwater kingdom of Atlantis. Huck rescues King Llandor of Atlantis from a clam. He is fascinated by the monarch's attire and vice versa so they exchange clothes. The henchmen of Morpho, King Llandor's treacherous minister (a.k.a. Injun Joe), mistake Huck for Llandor. Tom and Becky become Morpho's prisoners, but the youngsters get out his clutches and help Llandor stop Morpho and his minions.

Afterword

The New Adventures of Huckleberry Finn was not the last primetime animated program produced by Hanna-Barbera. In the summer of 1970, the studio came out with a new primetime cartoon, *Where's Huddles?* A replacement show for *The Glen Campbell Goodtime Hour* on CBS, it only lasted ten episodes and did not make the fall lineup. Then in 1972, Hanna-Barbera came out with another primetime cartoon, this time in syndication. *Wait Till Your Father Gets Home*, like *The Flintstones* and *Top Cat*, was inspired by a live-action sitcom, which in this case was *All in the Family*. This show actually ran two seasons but it failed to have a lasting impact. *Wait Till Your Father Gets Home* lacked *All in the Family*'s edginess and sharp satire. Nevertheless, one particular viewer was offended by the show. A California used car dealer named Cal Worthington was enraged by an episode about an unscrupulous car dealer. Contending that the character was an unfair lampoon of *him*, he sued Hanna-Barbera. Anxious to avoid any further legal battles, the studio became even more timid in handling controversial issues. Many local television stations felt *Wait Till Your Father Gets Home* lacked commerical appeal and didn't bother to air it. In the spring of 1982, NBC premiered *Jokebook* on primetime, consisting of comedy skits. Only three episodes were broadcast.

Throughout the 1970s and 1980s, Hanna-Barbera continued to devise primetime animated specials, particularly those reviving the eternally popular Flintstones. But the studio created most of its animation for the Saturday morning time slot. These programs were strictly marketed for children, not all ages like the 1960s primetime cartoons. Most of them only lasted one season although some of them would be rerun the following year. On the whole, Hanna-Barbera's cartoons were uninspired. They were intended to divert the little ones on the weekend. The tykes would then engage in other activities like outdoor play and forget what they had just watched.

Then in December 1989, a new primetime cartoon premiered on Fox. Created by Matt Groening, *The Simpsons* was an immediate smash hit with both critics and viewers. Like *The Flintstones*, the show focused on a blue collar family, headed by an overweight, lunkheaded but lovable lug. And like *The Flintstones*, this program was marketed for both children and adults. But *The Simpsons*'s humor was far more biting and sophisticated, not only because TV censorship standards had relaxed since the 1960s, but because Matt Groening was a satirist at heart. Bill Hanna and Joe Barbera wanted to please viewers and offend no one. Groening eagerly examined what he considered flawed about humanity and society, even if it meant ruffling a few feathers. But he used satire in an engaging and amusing way so people continued to enjoy the show. As of this writing, *The Simpsons* is still on the air and is now the longest running primetime cartoon.

The Simpsons's phenomenal success encouraged Fox and other networks to devise more primetime cartoons. Hanna-Barbera jumped on the bandwagon in early 1992 with two programs, *Capitol Critters* on ABC and *Fish Police* on CBS. If viewers hoped they would be hip and sly like *The Simpsons*, they were disappointed. Not only did these show go for easy laughs, but they lacked memorable protagonists. Critics weren't enthusiastic about the shows either. Long before the year's end, both shows were axed. To date, neither program has been revived.

Hanna-Barbera continued to function independently until 2001 when it was merged along with Warner Brothers by Time Warner. That same year, Bill Hanna passed away. Joe Barbera died in 2006. Since the merger, Hanna-Barbera's classic franchises like *Jonny Quest* have been marketed in new televison programs, theatrical movies and direct-to-video films. With the exception of *The New Adventures of Huckleberry Finn*, the 1960s primetime cartoons are still fondly remembered.

Even by the standards of the period they first aired, these programs weren't the most sophisticated or even the most clever cartoons on the airwaves. Jay Ward's *Rocky and His Friends* and Bob Clampett's *Beany and Cecil* boasted more cutting and mature humor. But there was a charming innocence about them. Whether they took place in the prehistoric past or the present or the distant future, these shows presented serene and charming environments where the inhabitants were generally considerate to each other and where problems, if they came up, were easily resolved. In the cases of *Jonny Quest* and *The New Adventures of Huckleberry Finn*, good always triumphed over evil.

More significantly, these shows had appealing characters one could identify with to a certain extent and care for. And as William Hanna pointed out, the characters cared about each other. There was a strong emotional bond in the families of *The Flintstones*, *The Jetsons*, and *Jonny Quest*. The characters in *The New Adventures of Huckleberry Finn* may not have been Mark Twain's characters, but the closeness and concern they expressed for each other seemed real. There was even mutual affection between Top Cat and his gang and Officer Dibble despite their ongoing battles. Hanna-Barbera's primetime cartoons of the 1960s were products of a more optimistic and idealistic time. Because of this these shows' warmth and sunniness, which enchanted both adults and children, can never be recaptured.

Bibliography

BOOKS

Barbera, Joe. *My Life in 'toons: From Flatbush to Bedrock in Under a Century.* Atlanta, GA: Turner Publishing, Inc., 1994.

Beck, Jerry. *The Flintstones: The Official Guide to the Cartoon Classic.* Philadelphia, PA: Running Press, 2011.

Blanc, Mel with Philip Bashe. *That's Not All Folks!: My Life in the Golden Age of Cartoons and Radio.* New York, NY: Warner Books, 1988.

Booker, M. Keith. *Drawn to Television: Prime-Time Animation From The Flintstones to Family Guy.* Westport, CT: Praeger, 2006.

Burlingame, Jon. *TV's Biggest Hits: The Story of Television Themes from "Dragnet" to "Friends."* New York, NY: Schirmer Books, 1996.

Erickson, Hal. *Television Cartoon Shows: An Illustrated Encyclopedia, 1949-2003, Volumes 1-2 . Second Edition.* Jefferson, NC: McFarland & Company, Inc., 2005.

Farley, Rebecca. "From Fred and Wilma to Ren and Stimpy: What Makes a Cartoon 'Prime Time'?" In *Primetime Animation: Television Animation and American Culture*. Edited by Carol A. Stabile and Mark Harrison. London and New York, NY: Routledge, 2003, 147-64.

Gitlin, Marty and Joe Was. *A Celebration of Animation: The 100 Greatest Characters in Television History*. Guilford, CT: Lyons Press, 2018.

Graydon, Danny. *The Jetsons: The Official Guide to the Cartoon Classic*. Philadelphia, PA: Running Press, 2011.

Hanna, Bill, with Tom Ito. *A Cast of Friends*. Dallas, TX: Taylor Publishing Company, 1996.

Lehman, Christopher P. *American Animated Cartoons of the Vietnam Era: A Study of Social Commentary in Films and Television Programs, 1961-1973*. Jefferson, NC: McFarland & Company, Inc., 2006.

Mallory, Michael. *Hanna-Barbera Cartoons*. New York, NY: Hugh Lauter Levin Associates, 1998.

Mittell, Jason. "The Great Saturday Morning Exile." In *Primetime Animation: Television Animation and American Culture*. Edited by Carol A. Stabile and Mark Harrison. London and New York, NY: Routledge, 2003. 33-54.

Perlmutter, David. *America Toons In: A History of Television Animation*. Jefferson, NC: McFarland & Company, Inc., 2014.

Sennett, Ted *The Art of Hanna-Barbera: Fifty Years of Creativity*. New York, NY: Viking Studio Books, 1989.

Spigel, Lynn. "White Flight." In *The Revolution Wasn't Televised: Sixties Television and Social Conflict*. Edited by Lynn Spigel and Michael Curtin. New York, NY: Routledge, 1997. 46-71.

ARTICLES

Amory, Cleveland. "Review: *The New Adventures of Huckleberry Finn.*" *TV Guide* (February 8-14, 1969): 36.

Fleming, Thomas J. "TV's Most Unexpected Hit." *Saturday Evening Post* Volume 234 Issue 48(December 2, 1961): 62-66.

Miller, Bob. "Walt Peregoy." *Animato!* Issue 22 (Winter 1992): 14-19.

WEBSITES

Classic Jonny Quest.com:http://www.classicjq.com/

Comfort TV:http://comforttv.blogspot.com/

Kiddiematinee.com:http://www.kiddiematinee.com/

Television Obscurities:https://www.tvobscurities.com/

Wikipedia:https://en.wikipedia.org/wiki/The_New_Adventures_of_ Huckleberry_Finn

Yowp: Stuff About Early Hanna-Barbera Cartoons:https://yowpyowp. blogspot.com/

VIDEO

"Jonny Quest: Adventures in Animation." *Jonny Quest: The Complete First Season: Hanna-Barbera Golden Collection*, disc 4, Warner Brothers, 2004. DVD.

Index

Made in the USA
Middletown, DE
24 July 2020